Cambridge Elements ≡

Elements in Music since 1945
edited by
Mervyn Cooke
University of Nottingham

A SEMIOTIC APPROACH TO OPEN NOTATIONS

Ambiguity as Opportunity

Tristan McKay

CAMBRIDGE
UNIVERSITY PRESS

CAMBRIDGE
UNIVERSITY PRESS

University Printing House, Cambridge CB2 8BS, United Kingdom

One Liberty Plaza, 20th Floor, New York, NY 10006, USA

477 Williamstown Road, Port Melbourne, VIC 3207, Australia

314–321, 3rd Floor, Plot 3, Splendor Forum, Jasola District Centre,
New Delhi – 110025, India

79 Anson Road, #06–04/06, Singapore 079906

Cambridge University Press is part of the University of Cambridge.

It furthers the University's mission by disseminating knowledge in the pursuit of
education, learning, and research at the highest international levels of excellence.

www.cambridge.org
Information on this title: www.cambridge.org/9781108813327
DOI: 10.1017/9781108884389

© Tristan McKay 2021

First published 2021

A catalogue record for this publication is available from the British Library.

ISBN 978-1-108-81332-7 Paperback
ISSN 2632-7791 (online)
ISSN 2632-7783 (print)

A Semiotic Approach to Open Notations

Ambiguity as Opportunity

Elements in Music since 1945

DOI: 10.1017/9781108884389
First published online: April 2021

Tristan McKay
Author for correspondence: Tristan McKay, tjm371@nyu.edu

Abstract: Along with twentieth-century developments in playing techniques, technologies, and concepts of musical sound, the notations employed by composers have also changed. Composers of what Umberto Eco calls "open works" often utilize intentionally ambiguous music notations. These open notations ask the performer to play a radical and active role in cocreating the musical work. In this text, I consider intersections of ambiguity, authority, and identity in works with open notations. Scores that feature open notations have been part of the Western classical music landscape since the mid-twentieth century, and continue to attract a vibrant community of practitioners today. I develop a semiotic approach to open notation analysis and put it into practice with in-depth analyses of works by Earle Brown, Will Redman, and Leah Asher.

Keywords: open notations, ambiguity, semiotics, open work, Earle Brown

ISBNs: 9781108813327 (PB), 9781108884389 (OC)
ISSNs: 2632-7791 (online), 2632-7783 (print)

Contents

Introduction

This Element is written as a foundational text in the study of ambiguous or open notations, through the lens of semiotics. Open notations have historically been called "graphic notations"; however, not all graphic notations are ambiguous and not all open notations are graphic. There is a tendency to position "graphic notations" solely as open and more picture-oriented rather than system-oriented. But this view of graphics is reductive and ineffective, as many graphics are able to capture great detail. Statistical graphics are extremely precise, as are engineering schematics or blueprints.[1] A graphic notation that shows sound events in time has the potential to be more specific than the most rhythmically intricate standard notations of complexity composers like Brian Ferneyhough (b. 1943) and Michael Finnissy (b. 1946). Graphics communicate information with many levels of specificity; this text is concerned with intentional ambiguity in music notation, and thus the term "open notation" is preferred.

I have made an effort to keep things as concise and as readable as possible, and although much of this text is centered on theory, my ultimate goal is practice-oriented. I wrote this with the assumption that the reader has a working knowledge of standard music notation and a foundational knowledge of classical music of the common practice period. Prior knowledge of semiotics and linguistics is not required, as the relevant theory is explained in depth in Section 2. Many of the examples discussed in this Element consider the point of view of the performer in learning and performing open notation repertoire. As I am a classically trained pianist who specializes in performing the music of our time, it should come as no surprise that many examples in this volume are considered on the piano, even when a given score might afford a more open instrumentation. Musical ideas embark upon a complex journey to travel from the mind of the composer to the minds of the audience, by way of the score and the performer. I focus on just one stage of this process: the quiet space between the performer and the score, where ideas are formed but sounds have not yet come into being.

In Section 1, I consider the problems and opportunities that open notations create for the performer. Because musical information is often presented in radically different ways in these scores, the performer cannot rely upon conventional interpretation. Semiotics sheds light on the interpretive act, ultimately enabling performers to craft interpretations of this repertoire with clarity and integrity. I consider the revolutionary work of Earle Brown (1926–2002) in the

---

[1] Edward R. Tufte, *The Visual Display of Quantitative Information* (Cheshire, CT: Graphics Press, 1983), 54–77.

1950s with *Folio* (1952–1953), and connect it to more recent pieces by Will
Redman (b. 1975) and Leah Asher (b. 1986); analyses of works by all three
composers are featured in Section 3.

In Section 1, I also articulate the philosophical and aesthetic position of open
notations by exploring the dynamic and ever-changing relationships among
composer, performer, and score. Umberto Eco argues that "the dialectic
between *form* and the *possibility* of multiple readings ... constitutes the very
essence of the 'open work.'"[2] The aesthetic value of openness is not restricted to
music notation. It is more broadly connected to ways of thinking about communication in the creation and reception of art. In works that take openness as
a primary aesthetic and compositional element, greater decision-making power
is granted to the performer. Open notations foster unique sites of creative
discourse and renegotiate traditional performer-composer relationships. The
identities of open works are also mediated by *Werktreue* and the work-
concept, which retain the position of the composer as sole author.[3] The score-
as-work also undergoes transformation through entextualization, the "process
of rendering a given instance of discourse a text."[4] Section 1 culminates in
a discussion of the relationship between the score-as-work (a rigid artifact) and
the score-as-discourse (a social space in flux).

In Section 2, I introduce four areas of semiotics that are central to my analyses
of open notations. First, I broadly consider the foundational work of Ferdinand
de Saussure[5] and C. S. Peirce.[6] Next, I examine perspectives on symbol systems
from Nelson Goodman[7] and John Kulvicki,[8] which support a view of notations-
as-systems. Third, I introduce the structural semiotics of Roman Jakobson[9] and
David Lidov,[10] with specific attention paid to notational syntax. Finally,

---

[2] Umberto Eco, *The Open Work*, translated by Anna Cancogni (Cambridge, MA: Harvard
University Press, 1989), 60.

[3] Lydia Goehr, "Being True to the Work," *Journal of Aesthetics and Art Criticism* 47, no. 1 (Winter
1989), 55–67.

[4] Greg Urban, "Entextualization, Replication, and Power," in *Natural Histories of Discourse*,
edited by Michael Silverstein and Greg Urban (Chicago: University of Chicago Press, 1996),
21–44 at 21.

[5] Ferdinand de Saussure, *Course in General Linguistics* [1916], new edition translated by
Roy Harris (La Salle, IL: Open Court, 1986).

[6] Richard Parmentier, *Signs in Society: Studies in Semiotic Anthropology* (Indianapolis: Indiana
University Press, 1994).

[7] Nelson Goodman, *Languages of Art* [1968], new edition (Indianapolis, IN: Hackett, 1976).

[8] John Kulvicki, "Analog Representation and the Parts Principle," *Review of Philosophy and
Psychology* 6 (2015), 165–180.

[9] Roman Jakobson, "Closing Statement: Linguistics and Poetics," in *Style in Language*, edited by
Thomas A. Sebeok (Cambridge: MIT Press, 1960), 350–377.

[10] David Lidov, *Elements of Semiotics: A Neo-structuralist Perspective*, 2nd edition (2017), 19.
https://davidlidov.com/about/elements-of-semiotics-2017/

I discuss the affordances of qualia and qualic transitivity, as developed by Nicholas Harkness[11] and Lily Chumley.[12]

In Section 3, I apply theory to practice in the analysis of works by Brown, Redman, and Asher. I consider the role of pitch content as symbol system in two works from Brown's *Folio*. Next, I examine Redman's use of three compositional tactics – *erasure, oversaturation,* and *extension* – in a page from his modular work *Book* (2006). Finally, I consider the roles of grammar and pattern, two syntactical frameworks, in crafting an interpretation of Asher's *TRAPPIST-1* (2017). As a set, these divergent works and their corresponding analyses show that notational ambiguity and openness are not trends of a bygone era, but compositional strategies that remain highly relevant today.

This Element is organized as a foundational text for scholars and students to use for their own semiotic analysis of open notations. As such, I include an appendix with a list of questions and prompts for approaching open scores with a semiotic eye.

1 Ambiguity as Opportunity

Like many young pianists, my first encounter with post-1945 Western classical music came surprisingly late in my studies. It wasn't until high school that my awareness extended beyond the too-common keyboard repertoire bookends of Johann Sebastian Bach (1685–1750) and Béla Bartók (1881–1945). The instructor showed the class some of George Crumb's (b. 1929) *Makrokosmos, Volume I* (1972), including "The Magic Circle of Infinity (Moto Perpetuo)" and "Spiral Galaxy" (Figure 1).

Crumb's dramatic notation in these movements piqued my curiosity about the ways in which notations organize and convey musical information to the performer. At the time, I had never seen anything like this score and was fascinated by how radically different it looked from the notations I knew. Most strikingly, the instructor made the claim that these notations – no matter how unfamiliar their shapes – are in fact quite conventional. The theatrical presentation of the spiraling staves does nothing to alter the information it conveys. Pianists who learn this repertoire, myself included, often take to these movements with scissors and tape to construct a more readable score. (Figure 2). In effect, this "straightening out" of the staves proves the point the

---

[11] Nicholas Harkness, *Songs of Seoul: An Ethnography of Voice and Voicing in Christian South Korea* (Berkeley: University of California Press, 2014).

[12] Lily Chumley and Nicholas Harkness, "Introduction: QUALIA," *Anthropological Theory* 13, no. 1–2 (2013), 3–11.

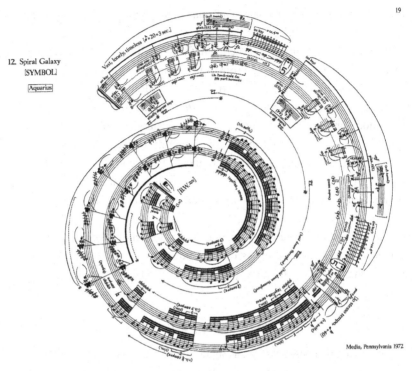

19

12. Spiral Galaxy
[SYMBOL]

Aquarius

Media, Pennsylvania 1972

Figure 1 George Crumb. "Spiral Galaxy," from *Makrokosmos, Volume I* (1972), p. 19

instructor was making – Crumb's poetic twisting of the staves is a stylish obstacle to what ends up being an unambiguous performance.

And yet I wonder if in altering the score, something is lost. Is it possible that even though the pitch, rhythm, and dynamic content of the original and reconstructed scores remain the same, that the reconstruction itself changes something fundamental about what the work communicates to the performer? In "Spiral Galaxy," the five-line staff curls inward in a clockwise direction, forming a spiral. And yet nothing about the spiral shape changes the content of what is on its staves. For example, the very first note is a low A that is both plucked with the finger tip – "pizz. (f.t.)" – and played on the key – "on key." Although Crumb also notates some extended techniques not commonly seen in keyboard repertoire, they are clearly articulated on the page and are wholly unambiguous.[13] In fact, all pitch material, rhythmic material, dynamics, articulation, and character markings are

---

[13] Extended techniques are approaches to playing a musical instrument other than those originally intended. Examples on the piano include tone clusters, plucking the strings of the piano, and muting the strings of the piano, among others.

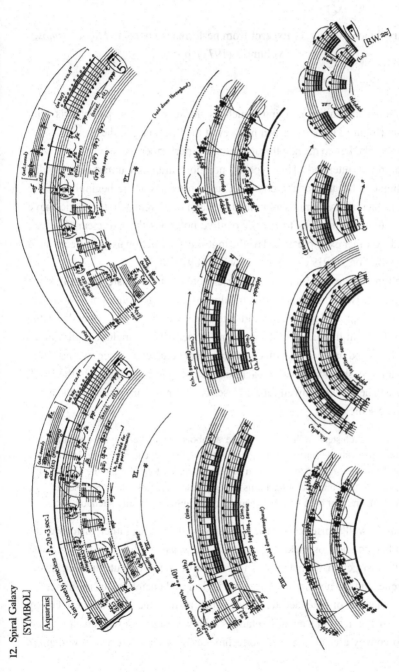

Figure 2 George Crumb. "Spiral Galaxy," from *Makrokosmos, Volume I* (1972), p. 19. Edited by Tristan McKay for performance.

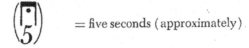

Figure 3 George Crumb. Excerpt from performance notes in *Makrokosmos*, Volume 1 (1972), p. 5

clear. Some unfamiliar markings, such as the number 5 in parenthesis with a square (Figure 3), are described in a key at the beginning of the score.

Without the key to decode this notation, the performer would not know what the composer intended. This type of notation, although unfamiliar, is also unambiguous because of the context Crumb provides at the beginning of the score. In fact, many composers in the twentieth and twenty-first centuries have taken it upon themselves to pen innovative notations that are clear and well defined. Another example would be the tone cluster notation used in pieces such as "Exhultation" (1919) by Henry Cowell (1897–1965).

The tone cluster notation (for a quarter note duration cluster) is a thick bar that connects two noteheads, vertically aligned. The noteheads at the lower- and uppermost points of the cluster indicate the lower and upper bounds of the cluster. Later in the piece, other durations appear. These include eighth notes (with flags) and half notes (with empty bars that connect between two half note noteheads). A sharp sign above each tone cluster indicates that only the black keys are to be played. Cowell further describes the notation in a short note at the top of the score:

> The tone clusters indicated by these symbols are to be played with the forearm, with the flat of the hand, or with the fist, depending on the length of the cluster. All the tones should be played exactly together and the pianist must see to it that the outer limits of the clusters are absolutely precise, as written, and that each tone between the outer limits is actually sounded.[14]

Without Cowell's instruction, the pianist would have to either disregard the unfamiliar notation or make an educated guess as to what it indicates. With Cowell's instruction, the pianist has a clear idea of how to execute the tone cluster technique, and the notation therefore has a clear and unambiguous meaning.

For notations of extended techniques such as this, the composer effectively extends the lexicon of standard notations with new signs. Cowell created a new sign to convey a clear and specific technique for which there was no notation.

---

[14] Henry Cowell, "Explanation of Symbols and Playing Instructions," in *Piano Music by Henry Cowell* (New York: Associated Music, 1960), back matter.

Over the past century of use, this notation became incorporated into a wider performance practice. Today, a pianist well versed in extended techniques should recognize the intended meaning of this sign without need of a key; it is part of a shared vocabulary.

1.1 Brown's *November 1952* and *December 1952*

Ingenuity does not necessitate ambiguity. Innovative or unfamiliar notations can be just as clearly defined as the body of notations associated with the five-line staff. The question remains: what constitutes ambiguity in music notation? The enigmatic *December 1952* by Brown provides one example. In this score, common elements of Western music notation such as the five-line staff, dynamic markings, and noteheads are completely absent. Instead, short vertical and horizontal lines of varying thicknesses are suspended in blank space on a single page (Figure 4).

These notations extend a great amount of openness to the performer in crafting an interpretation in practice. Without any of the usual notational

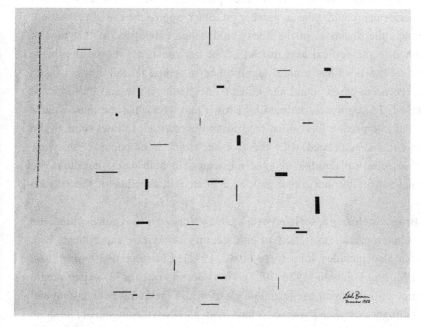

Figure 4 Earle Brown. *December 1952* from *Folio* (1952–1953)

conventions found within more standardized notation systems, works like *December 1952* pose a challenge to the performer: how do open notations represent or convey musical actions?

To interpret *December 1952*, a performer must decide how visual parameters relate to musical parameters such as pitch, duration, dynamic, timbre, and articulation. Even with abstract notations such as this, an unwritten expectation of consistency in their interpretation is common. For example, if a performer decides that the thickness of the lines in *December 1952* determines gradations of dynamic, then this rule should apply globally for every such line. *December 1952* is part of a larger set of works by Brown called *Folio*. The edition of *Folio* published by Associated Music compiles some of Brown's notes and writings on the pieces into a prefatory note. Brown gives some loose guidelines for interpreting *December 1952*, such as interpreting the score to have three dimensions (vertical, horizontal, and temporal), and assigning the thickness of each line to indicate the relative intensity (dynamic level) of the sound.[15] However, these notes are not guidelines so much as evidence of Brown's conceptualization of the piece at one moment in time. A performer could take a number of other approaches to the notation. Perhaps the thickness of the lines could indicate duration, so that time is aligned to the vertical axis instead of the horizontal. Or maybe the thickness of the lines has timbral significance in which thicker lines indicate a more noise-based sound and thinner lines indicate a sound that is more pitched. The approach outlined by Brown may seem like the most natural way of interpreting these notations, possibly because it follows some of the conventions associated with the five-line staff, a notational framework whose rules are familiar to most musicians; in both cases, durations are a function of the horizontal axis, and pitch is a function of the vertical axis.

Brown is closely associated with the New York school of composition, the defining musical institution of mid-century American experimentalism, which also includes John Cage (1912–1992), Christian Wolff (b. 1934), and Morton Feldman (1926–1987). He is best known for his experimental compositions, which use techniques and media including twelve-tone and Schillinger serialized music,[16] tape and electroacoustic music, graphic

---

[15] Earle Brown, "Prefatory Note," in *Folio (1952/53) and 4 Systems (1954)* (New York: Associated Music, 1961).

[16] The Schillinger System of Musical Composition, developed by Joseph Schillinger (1895–1943), was originally a four-year progression of classes taught through private instruction. The system is based on logical and mathematical concepts, and provides a structured approach to

notation, time notation, open form, and collage.[17] In "The Notation and Performance of New Music," Brown describes a turning point in his compositional practice in which he "came to a point of indicating rhythmic complexity and durational subtleties which seemed to [him] to be beyond counting and beyond performers' conscious or unconscious control of metric divisions on which standard notation is based."[18] In Brown's music, this complexity had developed out of his interests in the "total organization" of the Schillinger System and from generative principles that did not rely on a regular pulse or beat. In seeking a solution to this notational "problem," Brown drew upon concepts of mobility and immediacy from the work of visual artists Alexander Calder (1898–1976) and Jackson Pollock (1912–1956).[19] Calder's mobile pieces – simple geometric shapes suspended by wire and set in motion – are ever-changing structures. Pollock's "action painting" technique, used to create drip paintings such as *Mural on Indian Red Ground* (1950) and *Autumn Rhythm* (Number 30) (1950), captures the idea of mobility in a more embodied fashion. The final paintings, while static themselves, are very much about the artist's movement and choreography. Brown's notations in *Folio* (1952–1953) challenge conceptions of the score as a static artifact, and instead embrace transformation and variation.

December 1952 is perhaps the most recognizable work that uses open notations. The notation of *December 1952* is abstract in that it shares no commonalities with standard notations; it "is the graphic score often cited as an extreme pole in mid-twentieth-century, American avant-garde composition."[20] Brown wrote very few pieces with purely abstract graphic notations; others include *Hodograph I* (1959) and a number of one-page scores from *Folio II*, a collection of works written between 1970 and 2000 that remains unpublished.[21]

December 1952 is an example of what is often called "graphic notation." According to Brown, it is the earliest example, along with *November 1952* from the same set.[22] In *Notations in New Music*, Erhard Karkoschka

---

composition that transcends genre and aesthetic styles. The goal is to provide composers with broadly applicable solutions to compositional problems.

[17] Jason Cady, "An Overview of Earle Brown's Techniques and Media," in *Beyond Notation: The Music of Earle Brown*, edited by Rebecca Y. Kim (Ann Arbor: University of Michigan Press, 2017), 1–20.

[18] Earle Brown, "The Notation and Performance of New Music," *Musical Quarterly* 72, no. 2 (1986), 180–201 at 191.

[19] Earle Brown, "On December 1952," [1970; transcription of audio] *American Music* 26, no. 1 (Spring 2008), 1–12 at 1.

[20] Elizabeth Hoover, "Collage and the Feedback Condition of Earle Brown's *Calder Piece*," in *Beyond Notation: The Music of Earle Brown*, edited by Rebecca Y. Kim (Ann Arbor: University of Michigan Press, 2017), 159–187 at 163.

[21] Cady, "An Overview of Earle Brown's Techniques and Media," 6.

[22] Brown, "On December 1952," 7.

differentiates musical graphics from other notation types by their reliance upon graphic qualities to communicate information. He argues that unlike symbols,[23] which have a clear and defined content, graphic notations do not; their ambiguity can lead to any number of different interpretations.[24] Brown referred to this compositional quality as "creative ambiguity," in which a graphically notated piece leads to vastly different-sounding performances while maintaining its identity as an instance of the same work.[25] For Brown, ambiguity is an opportunity for creative engagement on the part of the performer. It is an aspect of composition and notation that is vital to the life of the work.

At the core of *December 1952* is Brown's preoccupation with mobility – movement, instability, and shifting structural relationships. His initial conception of the piece took the form of a box constructed with motorized parts. Vertical and horizontal elements inside the box would physically move during performance, and could be read as notation. When this idea proved to be mechanically impractical, Brown settled on a single-page score that presents something like "a photograph of a certain set of relationships of these various horizontal and vertical elements."[26] He substituted the physical mobility of his initial idea with a kind of conceptual mobility. The end result is a work that actively engages with the creativity of the performer, who must be deeply involved in deciding how to translate the notations on the page into musical sound.

1.2 Redman's *Book* (2006)

The notion of ambiguity as opportunity for creative engagement is not unique to Brown or the New York school; composers such as Redman continue to engage with these concepts in their creative practice.[27] Unlike many graphically notated pieces that feature notation devices created by the composer *ex nihilo* (such as those featured in the next Section on Asher's *TRAPPIST-1*), Redman mostly draws upon signs from the lexicon of standard notations. Redman's

---

[23] The word "symbol" here is a crude label signifying the body of notations related to conventional Western music notation. This use of the word lacks the specificity and significance of theory by Goodman and Peirce, which are discussed further in Section 2.

[24] Erhard Karkoschka, *Notation in New Music: A Critical Guide to Interpretation and Realization*, translated by Ruth Koenig (New York: Praeger, 1972), 3.

[25] Clemens Gresser, "Earle Brown's 'Creative Ambiguity' and Ideas of Co-creatorship in Selected Works," *Contemporary Music Review* 26, no. 3/4 (June/August 2007), 377–394.

[26] Brown, "On December 1952," 3.

[27] Much of the material in this Element on Redman was originally published in: Tristan McKay, "Graphic Notations As Creative Resilience in Redman's *Book* (2006)," in *Semiotics 2018: Resilience in an Age of Relation*, edited by Geoffrey Ross Owens and Elvira Katić (Charlottesville, VA: Philosophy Documentation Center Press, 2019), 157–171.

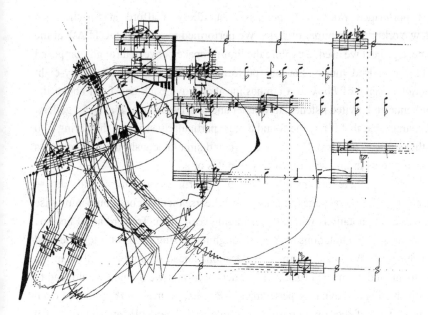

Figure 5 Will Redman. *Book* (2006), p. 3

biography states that his scores "employ fantastically unsystematic notation, inviting the beholder into a wilderness of interpretive self-sufficiency."[28] Instead of relying upon the conventional meanings of standard notation elements, Redman emphasizes other modes of semiotic engagement by presenting these familiar signs in alternative contexts (Figure 5).

I first came into contact with Redman's music during my graduate studies in the Contemporary Performance Program at the Manhattan School of Music, more specifically through the book *Notations 21*,[29] which prominently features a page from *Book* on its cover.[30] Theresa Sauer's anthology contains pages from an array of "illustrated musical scores" by more than one hundred international composers, among them canonized works by Karlheinz Stockhausen and Brown as well as less familiar works by emerging and mid-career composers.[31]

---

[28] Will Redman, "Short Bio," Will Redman official website (2010). Accessed December 17, 2019. www.willredman.com/short_bio.html.

[29] Theresa Sauer, *Notations 21* (New York: Mark Batty, 2009).

[30] The publication year of *Notations 21* (2009) marks the fortieth anniversary of John Cage's *Notations* (1969). Along with his coeditor, Alison Knowles, Cage used chance operations with the I-Ching to determine the order of the pieces as well as the typographical elements of the accompanying text. Sauer's volume similarly avoids organization into "types" of notation by ordering the pieces alphabetically by author's last name.

[31] Sauer, *Notations 21*, back matter.

I performed *Book* with percussionist Ellery Trafford at Spectrum in New York in the summer of 2013. We performed together as OUTLAW at the time, a project we used to explore the liminal space between through-composed and improvised music. For our performance, we fastened all ninety-eight modular pages of *Book* to a clothesline that wove back and forth above the audience and invited listeners to wander and observe them as if at an art gallery. We suggested that if anyone found a page particularly striking, they bring it to either of us to perform. We individually and simultaneously interpreted pages brought to us in this way for twenty minutes or so.

Certainly, there are many ways to perform *Book*. One could choose a selection of several pages and carefully rehearse them. Or one could improvise based on the notations without ever having seen them. Trafford and I became familiar with the notations of *Book* through rehearsing pages of it together and on our own. We made interpretive decisions ahead of time as well as in the moment, and we made organizational decisions that we thought would lead to an interesting and dynamic performance. Redman frames *Book* in such an open way that all of these readings are possible and acceptable, and more radical readings are even encouraged. Ambiguity is an essential component of Redman's compositional aesthetic.

In order to effectively analyze the notations in *Book* (in Section 3), we must consider the broader context of the piece. Because Redman does not include a clear guide for interpretation or performance for *Book*, a preliminary survey of some of his other graphic works is helpful for understanding how he wants his compositions to be conceived as works. Redman firmly establishes *Book* as an open work.[32] He grants the performer(s) as much freedom as possible while maintaining the status of the score as a primary and authored document. Authors of open works "propose a number of possibilities," or a "work to be completed" by the work's receiver.[33] Although the performer(s) may take many liberties with their interpretation, Redman claims that any performance of this piece will remain a performance of his work, rather than a free improvisation, a performance of some other piece, or a performance of no piece at all.

> *Book* (2006) is an unordered collection of 98 graphic compositions. The compositions represent extensions and extrapolations of conventional music notation and are available for use in any part, for any duration, by any number of performer(s), in any place, at any time. The notation and form are flexible enough to allow the performers' abilities and interest to have extraordinary influence over the interpretation of them. But no matter how radical the interpretation or what portions, quantities or combinations are

---

[32] "Open works," *Werktreue*, and general aesthetics are discussed in greater detail in Section 1.4.
[33] Eco, *Open Work*, 19.

used, the melodic, harmonic, textural, rhythmic and formal genetics of the composition as a whole remain evident.[34]

Similar to Brown (and many composers who use open notations), Redman does not consider ambiguity a problem, but an opportunity for creative engagement on the part of the performer. It is vital to the life of the work. Redman discusses the kind of interpretive openness he accesses through his notations.

> I was once told that not giving instructions was oppressive, and I thought that was kind of funny. I understood the point. Because the performer has this anxiety of the composer looking over and going "you got that wrong, you missed that." I didn't know how to express that once I finished the piece, I felt like giving it over . . . I like to take ownership of the fact that I made the score, but then I want the performers to take ownership of how it sounds. Another thing I say to performers is, I could tell you some things, but I'm hoping you have better ideas of how to play this than I do, because mine are pretty limited.[35]

In looking at several of Redman's other graphic scores, some common themes emerge. *Deck* (2013) resembles a deck of playing cards, with fifty-four card-sized scores. Similar to *Book*, *Deck*'s modularity allows performers to play the components individually or together, with the orientation of the score and the number of pages to be performed left to the performer's discretion.[36] Redman suggests that a game-like format can be used in performance, though it is not required. The score for *Scroll* (2011) is a single 8.5" x 88" piece of paper. Its notation is "fantastically unsystematic and confounds the composer at times."[37] He likens this notation to a kind of interpretive free fall, where the performer discovers what is salient. *Honoring Vertical Excellence* (2011) is a three-page score that presents the performer with variations on a four-line melody. His treatment of the notation varies from page to page. On one page, superimposed fragments of notation obstruct the melody; on the others, it is heavily orna-mented and annotated with dotted arrows that indicate nonlinear movement.[38]

In all of these open scores, Redman uses self-described "unsystematic nota-tions" and asks the performer to develop highly individual interpretations. He employs a variety of ambiguous compositional elements, such as unfamiliar

[34] Will Redman, "Book," Will Redman official website (2006). www.willredman.com/book.html.
[35] Will Redman, "Will Redman: Graphic Ideas in Sound," video interview by Molly Sheridan, *New Music Box* (blog) (July 27, 2011). Accessed December 17, 2019. https://vimeo.com/26929349.
[36] Will Redman, "Deck," Will Redman official website (2016). Accessed December 17, 2019. www.willredman.com/deck.html.
[37] Will Redman, "Scroll," Will Redman official website (2016). Accessed December 17, 2019. www.willredman.com/scroll.html.
[38] Will Redman, "Honoring Vertical Excellence," Will Redman official website (2011). Accessed December 17, 2019. www.willredman.com/hve.html.

notations without explanation and layered fragments of notation that are diffi-
cult to decipher. Despite the great amount of interpretive freedom he grants to
the performer, Redman defends the status of these scores as musical works
rather than unbounded improvisations. In the note for *Book*, he writes that the
musical genetics of the piece – melodic, harmonic, textural, rhythmic, and
formal elements – remain evident.[39] For *Scroll*, the sound may vary from performance to performance but is "musicogenetically" unified.[40] By drawing parallels
between compositional practice and genetic code, Redman suggests that the identity
of these works transcends their sound. Although performances of the same work
may not resemble one another, they are linked by virtue of their origin in the score.

1.3 Asher's *TRAPPIST-1* (2017)

Asher is a violinist, violist, composer, and visual artist based in New York.[41] In
2016, pianists Erika Dohi and Daniel Anastasio, cocurators of the BLUEPRINTS
Piano Series, approached me about performing a contemporary work at an
upcoming concert. With support from BLUEPRINTS, I co-commissioned
Asher to write a new piece for solo piano that related to the concert's theme of
"cosmology," which became *TRAPPIST-1*.

The score for *TRAPPIST-1* consists of seven movements (*b, c, d, e, f, g,* and *h*)
entirely written in graphic or open notation. The movements get progressively
longer, and vary from half a page to eight pages in length. Asher includes the
following prefatory note:

> *TRAPPIST-1* is named after the TRAPPIST-1 planetary system. The system
> consists of the star TRAPPIST-1a and seven known surrounding planets. The
> planets of TRAPPIST-1 have many earth-like characteristics that may or may
> not support living organisms. The movements of *TRAPPIST-1* are relative in
> length to the orbits of each of the seven planets.
>
> The performer may choose the order of movements. The performer is
> encouraged to use preparations on the piano and may vocalize or use found
> object instruments when they see fit.[42]

The score utilizes abstract, hand-drawn notations situated within a framework in
which the horizontal axis is time and the vertical axis is pitch (Figure 6).

It took a multistage process to bring *TRAPPIST-1* from its conceptual beginning to its premiere performance. I engaged with the score in a number of
different ways to generate, interpret, practice, and perform musical material

---

[39] Redman, "Book."

[40] Redman, "Scroll."

[41] Leah Asher, "Home Page," Leah Asher official website. Accessed December 17, 2019.
www.leahasher.com.

[42] Leah Asher, *TRAPPIST-1* (Independently published, 2017), prefatory note.

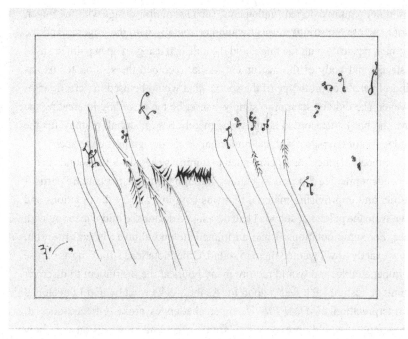

Figure 6 Leah Asher. *TRAPPIST-1* (2017), mov. g, p. 4

drawn from Asher's notations. She was initially interested in writing a piece that utilized unpitched and off-the-keys material on the piano, a goal complemented by my background in performing and commissioning works that utilize a wide range of extended techniques. Asher and I had a preliminary meeting in which I improvised at the piano. I brought a variety of playing implements for extended techniques including an ebow, lengths of bow hair, superball mallets, plectra, rubber tuning mutes, and a glass jar. As a pianist who specializes in contemporary classical music, I have amassed a sizeable collection of small objects to use for extended techniques at the piano. Some of these objects come from standard repertoire, such as a bent paper clip and set of glass rods used in Crumb's *Vox Balaenae* (1971). Other objects come from more recent pieces, such as lengths of bow hair and superball mallets used in David Bird's *IP(STROM* 2013). Still others are not connected to any notated works, but were collected for use in free improvisations, such as the rubber tuning mutes and glass jar. Before meeting with Asher, I selected objects from my collection that I was interested in using and that I believed would be in line with her vision of a piece that did not rely upon pitched material at the keyboard.

In our session, I improvised a wide variety of sounds, timbres, and gestures with these materials, somewhat guided by Asher. I also used extended techniques that did not require external implements, such as muting strings with the finger, scraping across the strings vertically and horizontally with the fingertip and the fingernail, pizzicato with the finger and the nail, and using an open palm to strike the strings and body of the instrument. Asher recorded the session for use as a kind of palette or prototype of the sounds that would be used in performance. However, she did not attempt to simply transcribe the recording in creating the score; the body of recorded sounds was merely base material, a study for the sound world of the piece, and had no formal or visual significance as such.

After receiving the score, I continued to improvise and discover sounds in my independent practice. I began by reading through the movements in no particular order and improvising material that was both inspired by the notations and drawn from the palette of sounds I had developed during the initial meeting with Asher. For some notations, I had an immediate and almost visceral reaction; I knew exactly how I wanted them to sound. Other notations struck me as obtuse and impenetrable, and would require many hours at the instrument to discover a sound or gesture I felt was a good fit. As the weeks went by and I developed my interpretation of *TRAPPIST-1*, other challenges arose. Often, issues of choreography would prevent me from executing my vision of how a movement should sound. For example, in the fourth page of movement *g* (Figure 6), there are a number of horizontal, thin lines.

I envisioned a thin, wispy glissando sound for this notation, which I created by pulling a glass jar along the strings of the piano while touching the activated strings with my free hand. This interpretation involves several layers of semiotic engagement. The reading of this notation as "thin" and "wispy" is an indexical reading of visual qualities, and the connection from visual qualia to the envisioned thin and wispy musical sound is an instance of qualic transitivity. This theory is discussed in greater depth in Section 2. Indexicality aside, this reading necessitates some discrepancies with the score. First, the diagonal lines often overlap on the horizontal axis (time), so that there is more than one at any given point. In order to create the glissando on the strings with the glass jar, both hands are required – one to pull the jar down the string, and one to pluck the string underneath it. As I played, I was not able to accommodate the overlapping nature of the lines with this technique, so I compensated in other ways. I sometimes would pluck the same string several times, or several different strings in succession, to create the illusion of overlapping glissandi – the illusion of iconicity between sounding performance and score.

Creating sounds for these notations was not a linear and systematic process, but rather an evolving and reflexive one. I often revised my interpretation of an earlier movement based on material I worked through in later movements. This usually happened with material that was visually related through some quality, yet distinct in other ways. I adapted my interpretation to accommodate the contrasting but related material. Chorcography proved to be a challenging component. In works like Crumb's *Makrokosmos I* (1972) and *II* (1973), extended techniques are specifically detailed in the score. Crumb's instructions account for the choreography required for the pianist to navigate between the keys and the inside of the instrument, so that adequate time is given to make the switches. In *TRAPPIST-1*, this work falls to the performer, as none of the playing techniques are specified in the score. Planning ahead is critical so as to minimize discrepancies with the notation and to successfully execute the intended choreography. In this way, extended technique choreography can restrict an interpretation from being more spontaneously conceived.

Even though time progresses in a linear motion from left to right as in a conventionally notated piece, it is not explicitly measured. Similarly, though pitch is expressed by the vertical placement of notation elements on the page, it is relative. Even within these constraints, there is openness and flexibility. Like Redman, Asher gives no further instruction as to how individual notations should be interpreted. Compositional elements such as repetition and variation and qualities such as density, thickness, and texture are visual indicators of structure. However, it falls to the performer to interpret these elements in musical terms and to build a consistent and meaningful sonic vocabulary and syntax.

1.4 Aesthetic Foundations

Open scores emphasize ambiguity as a central compositional or musical element, but this is not unique to these scores. Even the most "closed" and discrete score necessarily involves the human element of interpretation in performance.[43] Rather than supporting the binaries of open/closed and work/performance, I propose that open scores occupy a place at the intersection of these elements. In this Section, I introduce and discuss work by Eco and Goehr to establish the aesthetic foundations for the analysis in Section 3.

Eco is widely regarded as a key figure in semiotics, having published his first text on semiotics in 1968 with *La Strattura assente* and followed it with *A Theory of Semiotics* in 1975, among others. The main text I draw upon is *The Open Work*, a collection of Eco's pre-semiotic writings from the early to mid-1960s.[44] A substantial portion of this volume is comprised of *Opera Aperta* (1962), inspired by his contact with avant-garde artists and his study of the work of James Joyce; he was primarily interested in using his conception of the open

---

[43] See Panayotis Mavromatis, "A Multi-tiered Approach for Analyzing Expressive Timing in Musical Performance," in *Mathematics and Computation in Music*, edited by Elaine Chew, Adrian Childs, and Ching-Hua Chuan (Berlin: Springer, 2009), 193–204.

[44] Eco, *The Open Work*, 1–157.

work to bridge the gap he perceived between classical and modern art.[45] For example, Eco's exploration of the poetics of the open work begins with some musical examples, including one from Karlheinz Stockhausen. The notations in Stockhausen's *Klavierstücke XI* (1956) present the performer with different notation modules, which can be freely ordered at the discretion of the performer. Eco uses these pieces to illustrate how open works appeal to the initiative of the individual, as contrasted with the rigidity of definitive elements in classical compositions.[46]

Eco complicates this core idea with a few arguments. First, he acknowledges the openness that is inherent in the reception of all art; every reception is both an interpretation and a performance because of the fresh perspective that any act of reception entails.[47] Eco does not attempt to cast classical or older works as completely without variation in reception. Certainly, the individual experiences of audience members impact their reception of a work. Additionally, the performer-as-receiver for classical or more closed works is also confronted with degrees of openness. Variations in rhythm (expressive timing, rubato), dynamics (phrasing, shaping a melody), and timbre (shadings of articulation, layering of resonance) are central to any musical performance. For the "open work," however, openness is a salient and substantial element. In open musical scores, global elements such as pitch material may be left entirely open to the performer; a temporal openness might come from notations that can be played in any order. The decisions required in these cases are an outstanding feature of the score, not a byproduct of interpretation that is common to both open and closed scores. Eco focuses on interactions between art and viewer, while my focus is on the impact of musical notations on the performer.

"Openness" is distinct from "indefiniteness"; the affordances of any work are limited, and there are boundaries to their form, communication, and reception.[48] Eco states that "we can say that the 'work in movement' is the possibility of numerous different personal interventions, but it is not an amorphous invitation to indiscriminate participation. The invitation offers the performer the opportunity for an oriented insertion into something which always remains the world intended by the author."[49] Finally, he relates the quality of openness to the collaboration between author and receiver.[50] He defines the author as the one who "proposed a number of possibilities" or a "work to be completed," and the

---

[45] David Robey, Introduction to *The Open Work*, by Umberto Eco (Cambridge: Harvard University Press, 1989), ix.

[46] Eco, *Open Work*, 1–2.

[47] Eco, *Open Work*, 4.

[48] Eco, *Open Work*, 6.

[49] Eco, *Open Work*, 19.

[50] Eco, *Open Work*, 11–12.

interpreter as the one completing the work.[51] This orientation of the creative process around originator/completer and composer/performer returns repeatedly in discussions of what constitutes the open work.

Another central voice to this topic, Goehr is a musicologist and philosopher whose work focuses on the history of aesthetic theory, contemporary philosophy of the arts, critical theory, and philosophy of history. In *The Imaginary Museum of Musical Works*, she argues that in the early nineteenth century, musical activity was for the first time mediated primarily by the work-concept. In early chapters, she examines other ways of analyzing music (Nominalist and Platonist), and later critiques the extent to which they displace the ontological status of the music itself. For Goehr, "the major methodological transition is a move away from asking what kind of *object* a musical work is, to asking what kind of *concept* the work-concept is."[52] The development of oppositions such as composer/performer, absolute/programmatic music, and composition/improvisation contributed to the institutionalization of concert music and the formation of the so-called imaginary musical museum.[53] Ultimately, she calls upon us to question whether we "should continue to endorse the ideals associated with the work-concept, given its history and significance."[54]

"Conceptual imperialism" is to blame for the deeply embedded Romantic notion of the work-concept in the music production of the present. This has been an effort from two sides, with the institutional power behind musical infrastructure encouraging this practice, and composers and artists willingly adopting these institutional conventions to empower their own work.[55] The term *Werktreue*, or "being true to the work," is credited to E. T. A. Hoffman, who called for a separation of musical practice and extramusical considerations: "Thus, a musical work is held to be a composer's unique, objectified expression, a public and permanently existing artifact made up of musical elements."[56] The idea is not that pre-Romantic period composers did not compose works, but that their compositional practice was not regulated by the idea of a work-concept.[57] It is the dedication to *Werktreue* that distinguishes a performer who plays the open notation of a composer from a performer who improvises freely.[58]

---

[51] Eco, *Open Work*, 19.
[52] Goehr, *The Imaginary Museum of Musical Works*, revised edition (London: Oxford University Press, 2007), 90.
[53] Goehr, "Being True to the Work," 56.
[54] Goehr, *Imaginary Museum of Musical Works*, 9.
[55] Goehr, "Being True to the Work," 59.
[56] Goehr, "Being True to the Work," 55.
[57] Goehr, "Being True to the Work," 57.
[58] Goehr, *Imaginary Museum of Musical Works*, 263.

In some ways, the openness of open works poses a problem to the foundations of analytical work. Without clear guidelines to interpret notations, it could be argued, the performer may simply interpret without discretion. This concern can be approached from two directions. From a nominalist point of view, it is true that open scores are not considered notational. Nelson Goodman writes that "a score, whether or not ever used as a guide for a performance, has as a primary function the authoritative identification of a work from performance to performance."[59] In this way, any performance of a piece must be absolutely compliant with the notations of the score. Taken to its extreme, this argument would not consider the performance of a piece with a single wrong note to be a performance of that piece due to a discrepancy between the performance and the score. Goodman is not concerned with ideas of artistry or judgments of value (and certainly not with any notion of *Werktreue*), and notes that any performance, good or bad, that is absolutely compliant with the notations of the score is indeed a performance of the piece.[60]

Goehr provides an extensive critique of Goodman's theory of musical works, citing early music and avant-garde works, arguing that despite their notational openness, they retain an identity as works. "Many avant-gardists have tried to move away from the idea that two performances of a work should 'sound the same.' But from the fact that two performances do not sound the same it does not follow that they are excluded from being, in other respects, isomorphic or replicas of one another."[61] In other words, discourses surrounding performance "successes" extend beyond questions of accuracy. In opposition to Goodman, Goehr cites Alan Tormey, who argues that there are "conditions other than notational accuracy that help to preserve the identity of works."[62] In "Indeterminacy and Identity in Art," Tormey articulates his stance. The notion of "closed" and "open" works is somewhat of a fallacy, for no work can be fully determinate, and no work can be fully indeterminate.[63] As for questions of authorship, indeterminacy can be considered a compositional technique, not the absence of such: "It seems that we must insist, even against their protest, on crediting the employers of random techniques for the content of their productions, for their nihilistic desire to vanish gracefully from the scene is logically unattainable."[64]

Tormey poses an alternative to the nominalist notion of an isomorphic relationship between score and performance that Goodman demanded with

---

[59] Goodman, *Languages of Art*, 128.

[60] Goodman, *Languages of Art*, 186.

[61] Goehr, *Imaginary Museum of Musical Works*, 33.

[62] Goehr, *Imaginary Museum of Musical Works*, 34.

[63] Alan Tormey, "Indeterminacy and Identity in Art," *The Monist* 58, no. 2 (April 1974), 203–215 at 205.

[64] Tormey, "Indeterminacy and Identity in Art," 205.

what he labels "aleamorphic works."[65] Unlike the isomorphic view of works, in which a shared structural sameness between score and performance is required (score-performance model), aleamorphic works do not share this structural integrity. He suggests a rule-instantiation model as a replacement for Goodman's score-performance model, in which works are determined by the particular set of rules employed by the score:

> By adopting this rule-instantiation model we can accommodate all possible realizations of an aleagraphic work without concern for their mutual dissimilarities, for the identity of aleagraphic works does not depend on compliance with a character in a notational system (a score, for example) nor an isomorphism among such compliants, but on a polyadic relation among a set of sound events and a particular set of rules that are satisfied by those events.[66]

Tormey's work may be a prime alternative to the nominalist view on the integrity of performance, but I do not resort to delineating rule conditions or proofs for aleagraphic works. Rather, I accept the theory that Tormey and Goehr proposed as a philosophical and aesthetic grounding for open works so that I can do semiotic analysis. Open works remain works with a clear author, and they often require more involved participation on the part of the performer to complete. They are not strictly improvisatory, but they may involve improvisation.

At the beginning of this Section, I showed that Crumb's "Spiral Galaxy" from *Makrokosmos, Volume I* (1972) is in fact unambiguously, though quite unconventionally, notated. I introduced openly notated works by Brown, Redman, and Asher that engage with ambiguity in radically different ways. I developed an aesthetic foundation for analyzing these works with theory from Goehr and Eco. In Section 2, I delve into the deep well that is semiotics and cultivate a semiotic approach to analyzing open notations, and in Section 3, I return to the works by Brown, Redman, and Asher as case studies for analysis.

2 A Semiotic Approach to Open Notations

Semiotics is overflowing with potential applications to music notation, and more specifically to open notations. Out of the wide-ranging existing literature on semiotics, I concisely delineate four subsections that are particularly relevant for working with open notations. The first subsection (2.1) concerns the foundations of semiotics outlined by Saussure and Peirce, including their dyadic and triadic models of signification. The second (2.2) explores the symbol systems

---

[65] Tormey, "Indeterminacy and Identity in Art," 206.
[66] Tormey, "Indeterminacy and Identity in Art," 209.

theory of Nelson Goodman, as well as complementary texts by Kulvicki, Mitchell, and Urban. The third subsection (2.3) explores the structural semiotics of Jakobson, whose work Lidov later built upon. Finally, the fourth subsection (2.4) introduces Harkness and Chumley's work on qualia and qualic transitivity.

2.1 Semiotic Foundations

Saussure and Peirce developed their work contemporaneously but separately, in Switzerland and the United States, respectively. Saussure's model of signification is outlined in his *Course in General Linguistics*, a volume his colleagues compiled shortly after his death in 1913. Because Saussure left no unified written account of his theories, the editors have been blamed for a number of discrepancies in this text. As the book's translator, Roy Harris, notes, despite its secondhand construction, this is the authoritative text of Saussurean structuralism used by a generation of scholars, and there is "no convincing reason for supposing that it seriously misrepresents the kind of synthesis towards which Saussure himself was working when he died."[67]

Saussure proposed a dyadic form of signification that relates a signifier to a signified. One example of a signifier is the sound made by saying the word "tree." A corresponding signified would be the mental image of a tree in the mind of the perceiver. Another signifier for the same signified might be a photograph of a tree. In this case, the signified would be the same: a mental image of a tree. Saussure makes several claims that are common to Peirce's work, but these theories are not without their major differences. Saussure argues that, with the narrow exception of onomatopoeia, the relation of any signifier to a concept (or signified) is arbitrary.[68] The bonds that relate signifiers to signified are not arbitrary in their function on a cultural level, in the sense that the word "dog" relates to a similar concept for most speakers of English, but the specific sounds of the word "dog" are arbitrarily related to the concept. In Saussure's words, "a linguistic sign is not a link between a thing and a name, but between a concept and a sound-pattern."[69]

If the relationship between signifiers and signifieds is arbitrary, then how does culturally agreed upon meaning occur? For Saussure, the repeated associations between signifiers and signifieds within a system like a language become the process that creates and enforces bonds between them. A cyclical and self-reflexive process occurs between the two sides of Saussure's signification model: signifiers and signifieds are self-referential and trigger each other

---

[67] Saussure, *Course in General Linguistics*, xiii.

[68] Saussure, *Course in General Linguistics*, 67.

[69] Saussure, *Course in General Linguistics*, 66.

through their appearances in a system.[70] The more that speakers of English use the sound of the word "dog" to refer to the concept of a dog, the more the concept of a dog will be linked to the sound of the word "dog." In fact, Saussure argues that these bonds or values become so strong that individuals within a system (even those with greater political power in these matters, such as linguists) would be hard-pressed to change them. "A community is necessary in order to establish values. Values have no other rationale than usage and general agreement. An individual, acting alone, is incapable of establishing a value."[71]

Unlike Saussure, whose major contributions to semiotics are mostly drawn from his compiled lectures in *Course in General Linguistics*, Peirce was a prolific writer. During his lifetime, he published around seventy-five papers, twice that many book reviews, and no books. Peirce's writings covered a large swath of topics in the sciences (mathematics, geodesy, physics, chemistry, and astronomy) and the humanities (logic, philosophy, semiotics, metaphysics, cosmology, history of sciences, linguistics, lexicography, and psychology).[72] Following his death, his unpublished manuscripts – amounting to several hundred, excluding fragments – came into the care of the Department of Philosophy at Harvard University. These manuscripts are in various stages of completeness, with missing pages, absent dates, and some rewritten as many as a dozen times; for many documents, "it is often evident that Peirce himself was not able to select the final form."[73] These manuscripts were initially compiled into the six-volume *Collected Papers of Charles Sanders Peirce* in the 1930s, with two more volumes added in the 1950s. Together, these eight volumes contain twelve thousand pages of published papers.[74] A second compilation project, called the *Writings of Charles S. Peirce*, is currently underway, which aims to be selective but comprehensive and chronological. This project began with a group of Peirce scholars at Texas Tech University in the 1970s, later finding support from Indiana University, the National Endowment for the Humanities, and the National Science Foundation.[75] The eighth installment was published in 2009, with a projected thirty volumes for the complete project.

In "One, Two Three: Fundamental Categories," Peirce gives a compact overview of his semiotic triadic theory of firstness, secondness, and thirdness,

---

[70] Saussure, *Course in General Linguistics*, 66.

[71] Saussure, *Course in General Linguistics*, 112.

[72] The Peirce Edition Project, "Welcome to the Peirce Edition Project" (2015). Accessed December 17, 2019. http://peirce.iupui.edu/index.html.

[73] Charles S. Peirce, Charles Hartshorne, Paul Weiss, and Arthur W. Burks, *Collected Papers of Charles Sanders Peirce* (Cambridge, MA: Belknap Press of Harvard University Press, 1965), *CP*:1.iv.

[74] Joseph Brent, *Charles Sanders Peirce: A Life* (Bloomington: Indiana University Press, 1993), 9.

[75] The Peirce Edition Project, "History" (2015). Accessed December 17, 2019. http://peirce .iupui.edu/#history.

on a variety of levels in the semiotic process. Peirce outlines three fundamental elements of the signification process: sign, object, and interpretant. These elements function not as distinct entities, but as dimensions to the semiotic process.[76] The relationship among these three pieces of Peirce's theory allows for a variegated and nuanced analysis of signs and the signification process. On a fundamental level, Peirce's signification structure is similar to Saussure's in that it relates a sign (signifier) to an object (signified). However, a salient feature of Peirce's triadic theory is its focus on the interpretant (the mode of relation between sign and object) as fertile ground for an exploration of the diverse ways signification occurs. In fact, Parmentier makes the case that the object in Peirce's model is not related to the Saussurean concept of the signified, but that the "meaning" behind a sign in Peirce's model is found in the interpretant.[77]

The interpretant acts as "translation, explanation, meaning, or conceptualization" of the sign-object relationship.[78] Peirce considered a broad range of signs. Unlike Saussure, whose work focuses primarily on language and the systems of signs that form their underlying structures (what he called *langue*), Peirce's conception of the sign included "whatever is adapted to transmitting to a person an impression that virtually emanates from something external to itself."[79] The inclusiveness in Peirce's definition of signification, coupled with his focus on the interpretant as fundamental to the process, prompted a number of sign classes.

Peirce conceives three hierarchically nested sign classes: icon, index, and symbol. An icon relates to its object "by virtue of some resemblance or similarity" with it (firstness); an index relates to its object through "some actual or physical or imagined casual connection" (secondness); a symbol relates to its object as a matter of "social convention" (thirdness).[80] The orientation of symbol as "social convention" directly relates to Saussure's conception of the arbitrariness of the sign; with nothing inherent to the sign to connect it to its object (like an icon), or to its interpretant (like an index), connection is built from a socially or culturally agreed upon convention underlying its signification. In this way, all symbols are necessarily arbitrary, whereas icons and indexes are in some capacity regulated. The symbol is the only sign type that is necessarily triadic; its dependence upon all three parts of Peirce's model of signification renders it the most complex but also the most adaptable to a broad range of signs.

[76] Parmentier, *Signs in Society*, 9–10.
[77] Parmentier, *Signs in Society*, 10.
[78] Parmentier, *Signs in Society*, 5.
[79] Parmentier, *Signs in Society*, 3.
[80] Floyd Merrell, "Charles Sanders Peirce's Concept of the Sign," in *The Routledge Companion to Semiotics and Linguistics*, edited by Paul Cobley (London: Routledge, 2001), 28–39 at 31.

In sharp contrast to Saussure, Peirce embraces the elaborate and varied nature of the signification process. The flexibility of his triadic model allows for mobility, transformation, and greater subjectivity in describing signification. For example, Peirce's model is able to account for multiple interrelated moments of signification. In the triadic modeling of a sign, the interpretant can become the sign for a new act of signification. Complex events with multiple semiotic sites give way to multilayered triadic models that can be chained together to show a progression in time. Rather than estimating an idealized system out of time, Peirce's model is necessarily time-dependent. In this way, Saussure's model is more prescriptive in that it creates a signification model out of time and attempts to fit events into it, whereas Peirce's model is descriptive in that it approaches a nuanced and subjective reading of signification with a model that adapts to fit the situation.

The relationship between the theories of these two thinkers is complex; much of Saussure's work supplies a clear base for Peirce's work, which emphasizes the importance of perception and the individual by way of interpretant. In analysis, the interpretant can be elusive. It often may seem like the interpretant is absent in cases where meaning is familiar and naturalized. This goes for symbols for which the culturally mediated code is deeply engrained in us, where the interpretant feels immediate and without variation.

Peirce makes another significant distinction in his classification of signs: sinsigns are signs that have no other existence except as signs. Legisigns, by contrast, are signs that have a definitely significant form, so that an overarching law mediates instances of the sign.[81] Sinsigns are also called "tokens," and legisigns "types." A specific instance of a legisign (sinsign) is a "replica."[82] While all legisigns are necessarily sinsigns, not all sinsigns are necessarily legisigns.

This difference is evinced in music notation with the pitches indicated by notes on the staff. When a musician experienced in reading conventional Western notation sees a note on the staff, they without hesitation understand what note to play. The system of lines and spaces on the staff allows for a symbolic reading of the note so that there is no doubt as to what pitch it is; the interpretant for a symbolic reading is dictated by the system to which it belongs. This reading relies upon conventions attributed to the signs as legisigns, and the type-distinction that enables consistent interpretation (or replicas) across performances.

A nonmusician or musician experienced in another notation system may have a completely different encounter with this sign. Perhaps they see it simply as

---

[81] Parmentier, *Signs in Society*, 7–8.
[82] Parmentier, *Signs in Society*, 7–8.

signifying music notation itself, or a single note, or indecipherable ink on a page – all examples of sinsigns, or immediate engagement with the sign as it exists without an overarching code. Different sign-objects are accessed by way of different interpretants. In my work with open notations, the interpretant is the central site of analysis. The instability of these signs asks for an analysis that examines possibilities, rather than actualities. Interpretants that point to iconic and symbolic modes are easier to pinpoint, as they rely upon a culturally grounded or actual/causal connection. Interpretants that point to indexical modes, as is often the case with open notations, are slippery; they point to arrays of rather than to individual sign-objects.

2.2 Symbol Systems

Goodman was an American philosopher and aesthetician known for his wide-reaching work from mathematics and formal logic to the philosophy of science and art. In this subsection, I introduce some elements of his scientific and taxonomic approach to aesthetics. I complement his approach with revisions and parallels by Kulvicki, W. J. T. Mitchell, and Greg Urban.

In *Languages of Art*, Goodman outlines and defines analog and digital symbol systems. His account of analog and digital refers not to singular instances of symbols, but to entire systems of symbols. In this way, one would not consider a single symbol as analog or digital, but the system to which it belongs. According to Goodman, an analog symbol system must be syntactically and semantically dense.[83] A symbol system is syntactically dense if and only if for any two symbols, a third lies between. For example, consider a chart that shows the fluctuating height of a mercury thermometer over time, as represented by a continuous line where the x-axis shows time and the y-axis shows temperature. Assuming this line is continuous, every point on the line is syntactically distinct in that between any two points a third is possible. In other words, any distinct point selected on a continuous line inscribes a unique symbol. A symbol system is semantically dense if and only if for every character there is a continuous (not disjoint) offering of other possibilities. In the chart example, this is evident in the possible vertical placement of any point. In measuring the height of the mercury in a thermometer, there are a continuous and infinite number of possible heights that each point could represent. While the mercury in a thermometer is bound by the upper and lower limits (perhaps from 0°C to 100°C), this poses no threat to the semantic density of the system itself; the *field of referents* for the symbols exhibits a semantic density.

---

[83] Goodman, *Languages of Art*, 160.

In addition to syntactic and semantic differentiation, Goodman's definition of digital systems requires discontinuity.[84] Discontinuity implies the clear division of each symbol from all others. If the temperature chart were revised to measure data in a more limited way, it could exemplify a digital system. For example, such a chart might plot only twenty-four points that represent the temperature measured every hour over the course of a day on the x-axis, with the temperature measured in ten-degree blocks such as 0–10°C and 10–20°C on the y-axis. The twenty-four points presented on the chart remain separate and distinct from all others, and in turn it is not always true that for any two points a third would lie between. For example, if the two points selected were for hours 1 and 2, there would not be a third point plotted between them.

A substantial part of *Languages of Art* applies these systems to different artistic media and discusses their aesthetic implications. In relation to music notation, Goodman argues that notations are fundamentally digital symbol systems and outlines the requirements for such a system to actually notate. For a symbol system to be notational, it must rely upon "compliance classes" that are consistent across the notational system. "In sum, the properties required of a notational system are unambiguity and syntactic and semantic disjointedness and differentiation."[85] These are not merely recommended for a good and useful notation, but are features that distinguish notational systems – good and bad – from systems that are non-notational. Goodman argues that a musical score, acting as a notational system, preserves the definitive and genuine identity of a musical work upon which all performances are measured. Only through complete compliance with the score is a genuine performance of a work possible.[86]

Kulvicki critiques and revises Goodman's concept of analog symbol systems in "Analog Representations and the Parts Principle." Kulvicki is a philosopher whose work focuses on perception – more specifically, how perceptual states interact with our environment, and the phenomenology of perception as a sensory experience. His other work, such as the article cited here, focuses on the nature of pictorial representation and considers the relationships among diagrams and representations, pictures, and realism. He critiques Goodman's conception of the analog as an essentially "smooth" feature of symbol systems. By smoothness, he refers to Goodman's requirement of syntactic and semantic density. Kulvicki describes this as an orientation grounded in an "engineering" mentality rather than an "interpretive" one in that the analog distinction makes sense from the point of view of

---

[84] Goodman, *Languages of Art*, 161.

[85] Goodman, *Languages of Art*, 156.

[86] Goodman, *Languages of Art*, 186.

systematic analysis, but not in a way that involves actual interpretation.[87] While it may be true that for a mercury thermometer we can never read the exact height of the mercury but only an approximation, we do not in practice need to conceive of infinite readings when we engage with analog systems. Similarly, we never wonder when we look at a clock whether the minute hand is indicating 4.567 minutes or 4.568 minutes or 4.5675 minutes – rather, we notice that it is around 4 minutes, or between 4 and 5 minutes, and this is meaningful enough. Thus Kulvicki integrates his idea of "degrees of roughness" into a reading of analog symbol systems. He argues that through the abstraction of structural elements, analog systems make many levels of structural information available to interpreters at any given moment.

More specifically, Kulvicki posits that the varying degrees of roughness available to interpreters of analog systems, coupled with an isomorphic relationship between systems of marks and their representations, allow for "open-ended searches for content, across levels of determinateness – in virtue of their syntactic and semantic structures."[88] These open-ended searches grant interpreters access to information about structural content for various resolutions or abstractions,= of a given symbol system. Open-ended searches are only possible because of an inherent structural preservation in the given symbol system. When "approximations to a representation's syntactic identity are readily mapped onto approximations to its semantic identity," this is feasible.[89] There is an isomorphic relationship between syntactic and semantic qualities and their corresponding representations. An example of this isomorphic relationship is found between the numbers on a pressure gauge and the pressures it is measuring. In this case, the distance between numbers on the pressure gauge is isomorphically linked to the pressure of the chamber that the gauge is measuring. Because of this relationship, even a quick flick of the dial's hand indicates a change in pressure paralleled in the chamber. Without the isomorphic mapping of pressure to space on the meter, this kind of judgment would not be possible at first glance.

Kulvicki broadens the analog concept to include systems without continuity, or "smoothness." He posits that despite the lack of smoothness, such systems offer interpreters the possibility of open-ended searches as a result of the isomorphic relationship. "Abstractions over the syntactic qualities map readily onto abstractions over the content, and so the content is only articulable as spanning levels of abstractions."[90] Abstractions result from varying degrees of

[87] Kulvicki, "Analog Representation and the Parts Principle," 165.
[88] Kulvicki, "Analog Representation and the Parts Principle," 166.
[89] Kulvicki, "Analog Representation and the Parts Principle," 169.
[90] Kulvicki, "Analog Representation and the Parts Principle," 175.

roughness used in reading a symbol system. Roughness can be illustrated by the depiction of color with various resolutions of a digital image. At a very high resolution, color arrays are very finitely differentiated from one another. At a low resolution, larger structures of color relationships are depicted by larger pixel size. A rougher reading of the high-resolution image would extract from it only content that the lower-resolution image would share; the larger pixels would be identical to abstractions of the same resolution of the more finitely differentiated pixels in the higher-resolution image. Ultimately, Kulvicki argues that for what Goodman calls digital symbol systems to be read as analog, opportunities for open-ended searches across levels of abstraction must outnumber the needs of ordinary users in ordinary contexts of use.[91]

Goodman's conception of symbol systems is further explored by Mitchell in "Pictures and Paragraphs: Nelson Goodman," part of a larger book on intersections of image, text, and ideology in the work of philosophers, aestheticians, and semioticians.[92] Mitchell is an art historian and editor of the interdisciplinary journal *Critical Inquiry*. His research considers the history and theories of media, visual art, and literature from the eighteenth century to the present, through the lens of representation and iconology. While Mitchell acknowledges the potential for Goodman's work to be seen as quite aggressive, political, and exclusionary, he emphasizes Goodman's "Olympian neutrality" on matters of political, artistic, and philosophical intent.[93] In many ways, Mitchell praises Goodman's taxonomic and nominalist work with signs, calling it the "Occam's razor we need for cutting through the jungle of signs, so that we may see just what sort of flora we are dealing with."[94] Mitchell's focus is on Goodman's contributions to the conversation on text-image sign theory. He reminds us that Goodman's work allows for hybrid works, in which a sign system can be read as a picture or as a description depending on the mode of reading employed.[95] "The mode of reading is regularly a matter of habit, convention, and authorial stipulation – thus, a matter of choice, need, and interest."[96] These highly contextual, perceptual, and individual elements fall outside of Goodman's theory; although Goodman may account for multiple modes of reading with a single text, he does not extend his work to consider the human element in signification.

---

[91] Kulvicki, "Analog Representation and the Parts Principle," 175.

[92] W. J. T. Mitchell, "Pictures and Paragraphs: Nelson Goodman," in *Iconology: Image, Text, Ideology* (Chicago: University of Chicago Press, 1986), 47–74.

[93] Mitchell, "Pictures and Paragraphs," 71.

[94] Mitchell, "Pictures and Paragraphs," 63.

[95] An example of this is concrete poetry, which blurs the line between text as description and text as image. See Barrie Tullett, *Typewriter Art: A Modern Anthology* (London: Laurence King, 2014).

[96] Mitchell, "Pictures and Paragraphs," 70.

Another linguistic process at work in open scores is that of entextualization, the "process of rendering a given instance of discourse a text."[97] When texts are replicated, as is the case with transcription as shown by Urban in "Entextualization, Replication, and Power," there is an attempt at reproduction that involves the original and copied discourse as well as the social relationships between the originator and copier.[98] With open notations, there are two levels of text: the score created by the composer and the performance created by the interpreter of the score. In performing an open work, the player engages with the score as a richly entextualized document and contributes new layers of meaning to the identity of the work. The original text itself (the score) generally remains the same. It is the ontological identity of the work in the world, the sum of all its parts (performances, recordings, etc.), that is changed. Yet open works are not born into this state; entextualization is the process of something becoming recognized as that object. The discourse surrounding these texts is in a constant state of flux. A performance is not a mere copy of the original, but an active contribution to an ever-changing dialogue. The process of works "becoming" is evidence of the creativity of the performer, whose actions not only respond to the work proposed by the composer but also actively contribute to its identity. The entextualization of the open work erodes the "conceptual imperialism" that has calcified music of the past three centuries. The status of the open work as a text-in-motion disrupts the authorial power of the composer and extends its identity to include layers of meaning, interpretation, and discourse contributed by the performer.

The originator (composer) can also build entextualizing cues into the original work to guide the replication or transcription by the copier (performer).[99] These cues also serve as guidelines for what is and is not considered a replica of the original. The interpretation of a musical score is a cross-modal action, as visual signs are converted into musical sounds. In many works with open notations, cues can be as obvious as a key for interpreting unconventional signs or a set of instructions included with the score. Other cues may be less obvious, or even unintentional side effects of the medium. For example, temporal limitations may be implicit but not explicit. In *TRAPPIST-1*, the lengths of the movements (by number of pages) should correspond to their relative duration, though no specific duration is specified in smaller divisions. In this way, entextualization can be viewed not just across different interpretations of the same text but also within a singular interpretation. Whether the performer takes time to develop a rich and detailed reading of the score-as-text or improvises an interpretation, each singular

[97] Urban, "Entextualization, Replication, and Power," 21.
[98] Urban, "Entextualization, Replication, and Power," 21.
[99] Urban, "Entextualization, Replication, and Power," 42.

performance enacts entextualization. Performers may draw upon moments of discourse outside of the text such as recordings or records of past performances of works, some of which remain significant while others are forgotten. Entextualization cues in a score may be meaningful, but also previous responses to the cues from other performers may become conventionalized as performance practice. When an open score is replicated as a text in performance, all of these sites of discourse can factor into that moment of entextualization.

2.3 Structural Semiotics

Jakobson coined the term "structuralism" in 1929 to indicate "an analytical method which involves the application of the linguistic model to a much wider range of social phenomena."[100] In anthropology, Claude Lévi-Strauss argues that deep logical structures are universally shared across cultures.[101] I instead use structural semiotics to look at syntactical structures of individual works and make no claims about cross-cultural deep structures or universals.

The early semiotics work developed in Saussure's *Course in General Linguistics* was largely structural, as Saussure "wanted a standpoint for a disciplined analysis of language."[102] One of the main tenets of his work is the distinction between two branches: static linguistics and evolutionary linguistics.[103] Saussure proposes an axis orientation in which the x-axis represents the *axis of simultaneity*, which considers "relations between things which coexist, relations from which the passage of time is entirely excluded," and the *axis of succession* on the y-axis, which considers only one thing at a time, over time.[104] Static linguistics is concerned with the axis of simultaneity. With time removed from the equation, linguistic structures can be analyzed and explored without considering historical precedent or the possibility of change; this work is concerned with things as they are. Evolutionary linguistics is instead focused on the evolution of structural elements through time; focusing on one element allows the various changes it experiences to be examined in relative isolation.

Jakobson continued Saussure's structural work. As a principal founder of the Prague school, Jakobson was a major figure in the European movement in structural linguistics. He is best known for his work with phonemes and the structure of phonological systems. In "Closing Statement: Linguistics and Poetics," he delivers his thoughts on the relation of poetics to linguistics. He

---

[100] Daniel Chandler, *Semiotics: The Basics*, 2nd edition (London: Routledge, 2002), 5.
[101] Claude Lévi-Strauss, *Structural Anthropology, translated by Claire Jacobson and Brooke Grundfest Schoepf* (New York: Basic Books, 1963).
[102] Lidov, *Elements of Semiotics*, 19.
[103] Saussure, *Course in General Linguistics*, 79.
[104] Saussure, *Course in General Linguistics*, 80.

writes that poetics "primarily deals with the question *'What makes a verbal message a work of art?'"*[105] Through the filter of his theory of message construction, he arrives at the argument that the *poetic function* is the dominant function of verbal art.[106] His model of message construction has six components, contrasted with the two of Saussure and the three of Peirce:[107]

> The ADDRESSER sends a MESSAGE to the ADDRESSEE. To be operative the message requires a CONTEXT referred to (referent in another, somewhat ambiguous, nomenclature), seizable by the addressee, and either verbal or capable of being verbalized; a CODE fully, or at least partially, common to the addresser and addressee (or in other words, to the encoder and decoder of the message); and finally, a CONTACT, a physical channel and psychological connection between the addresser and addressee, enabling both of them to enter and stay in communication. All these factors inalienably involved in verbal communication may be schematized as follows:

$$
\begin{array}{c}
\text{CONTEXT} \\
\text{ADDRESSER} \ldots \ldots .. \text{MESSAGE} \ldots \ldots .. \text{ADDRESSEE} \\
\text{CONTACT} \\
\text{CODE}
\end{array}
$$

Jakobson's notion of the poetic function relies upon an axis orientation of message construction: the axis of combination (semantics) on the x-axis and the axis of selection (syntax) on the y-axis. This model is a direct extension of the axis model proposed by Saussure, though it is applied to message construction rather than branches of linguistics. Jakobson's key argument is that "the poetic function projects the principle of equivalence from the axis of selection into the axis of combination."[108]

The principle of equivalence in the axis of selection is easily explained using adjectives. In the sentence "It's cold outside," the adjective "cold" could easily be replaced with a number of variations: chilly, brisk, freezing, or frigid. These terms are equivalent in that they communicate a similar idea concerning the state of the weather. In projecting the principle of equivalence into the axis of combination, as seen in poetry, equivalence is also present in syntax. Syntactical structures in poetry organize elements such as nouns, syllables, and meter in ways that prosodic speech generally does not. "This is not to say that in prose there are no parallelisms or repetitions or any other of the devices particularly associated with poetry; but rather to say that such symmetries are not the constructive device of

---

[105] Jakobson, "Closing Statement," 147.
[106] Jakobson, "Closing Statement," 153.
[107] Jakobson, "Closing Statement," 150.
[108] Jakobson, "Closing Statement," 155.

prose and are not as systematically used."[109] Jacobson's concept of poetic function is key to understanding how open notations do the job of notating. In Peircean terms, these signs are indexical, as they point to relationships among visual and aural qualities. In a score, this could be something like the "sharpness" of a line pointing to a sharp or harsh timbre, the jaggedness of a musical line, or the shortness of a note's duration. In this example, I use poetic textual descriptions to approximate visual qualities of a notation and aural qualities of a musical sound. The principle of equivalence shows connections among these descriptors, as it does for their corresponding visual and aural qualities.

Lidov extends the structuralist view on syntax that began with Saussure's work in *Course in General Linguistics* and continued with the work of Jakobson and Chomsky. Lidov is a composer whose scholarly work examines issues around musicology and semiotics, specifically the capacities of different media for reference and structure. His areas of research include metrical theory, general semiotics, and applications of semiotics to music. Claiming that Jakobson's work is unable to distinguish between structure of language as a system and structure found in individual works, he builds upon a series of articles by linguist and musicologist Nicolas Ruwet.[110] *Pattern* and *grammar* are two sides of what he calls "double syntax," which together produce "radically individual" interactions.[111] This approach to syntax addresses the issue Lidov raises with Jakobson's work by reconciling large-scale and localized syntax: "It is meant to rectify or clarify the theory underlying [Jakobson's] method."[112] The concept of *double syntax* is situated at the crossroads of *grammar* with deep structure and *pattern* with surface structure.[113] "A grammar is a set of rules governing abstract categories[114] (such as 'noun' in language or 'diagonals' in chess) and combinations of their elements, and the grammar of a text can refer to the structure it exhibits as an example fitting those rules."[115] Pattern, by contrast, "is a structure that can be discovered in one text in isolation ... patterns suggest categories and rules, but these are immediate consequences of the text which exhibits them, without the *a priori* status they would hold in a grammar."[116]

---

[109] Linda Waugh, "The Poetic Function in the Theory of Roman Jakobson," *Poetics Today* 2, no. 1a (Autumn 1980), 57–82 at 64–65.

[110] See Nicholas Ruwet and Mark Everist, "Methods of Analysis in Musicology," *Music Analysis* 6, no. 1/2 (March–July 1987): 3–9, 11–36.

[111] Lidov, *Elements of Semiotics*, 161.

[112] Lidov, *Elements of Semiotics*, 163.

[113] Lidov, *Elements of Semiotics*, 163.

[114] Also referred to as "paradigms," which concern semantics as on Saussure's axis of simultaneity and Jakobson's axis of equivalence.

[115] Lidov, *Elements of Semiotics*, 88.

[116] Lidov, *Elements of Semiotics*, 89.

Grammatical *categories* are "collections of possible constituents ... that are known to us but usually not all present to us; they are collections *in absentia*, and strictly in that sense abstract."[117] A grammatical category holds a single place on Jakobson's axis of combination but appeals to the possibilities afforded by the axis of selection. "A combination – a syntagm – that realizes a grammatical rule is a *form*."[118] Since pattern is grounded in a specific work, and does not need to appeal to the endless possibilities afforded by abstract grammatical categories and forms, some different elements are present in analysis. *Sets* are "paradigms determined by similarity and contrast within one text."[119] "Syntagms determined by adjacency, parallelisms, and segmentation are called *units*."[120]

I consider a structural approach to syntax in my analysis of Asher's *TRAPPIST-1* in Section 3.3, specifically through the lens of grammar and pattern. In the next section, I introduce qualia and qualic transitivity, ideas that Harkness and Chumley developed out of earlier work by Munn. I mainly consider the roles of qualia and qualic transitivity in relation to the indexical signification of open notations, a thread that runs throughout my this text but is discussed in detail in Section 3.2 on Redman's *Book*.

2.4 *Qualia* and *Qualic Transitivity*

Semiotic anthropology developed out of the work of Milton Singer in the late 1970s at the University of Chicago, where it has continued to be an area of special interest.[121] Scholars such as linguist Michael Silverstein, a colleague of Singer's, as well as his students Lily Chumley and Nicholas Harkness, have continued to use semiotics as a vital theoretical foundation for their research. Harkness and Chumley coedited a special issue of *Anthropological Theory*, which presents ethnographic studies informed by Peirce's concept of qualia. Qualia are "experiences of sensuous qualities (such as colors, textures, sounds, and smells) and feelings (such as satiety, anxiety, proximity, and otherness)."[122] In the introduction to this issue, Chumley and Harkness attribute the familiarity of Peirce's term "qualisign" to anthropologist Nancy Munn's *The Fame of Gawa*.[123] Munn examines the production of qualisigns such as darkness, heaviness, and buoyancy in relation to cultural practices.

---

[117] Lidov, *Elements of Semiotics*, 164.
[118] Lidov, *Elements of Semiotics*, 164.
[119] Lidov, *Elements of Semiotics*, 165.
[120] Lidov, *Elements of Semiotics*, 165.
[121] University of Chicago, "History," Department of Anthropology. Accessed December 17, 2019. https://anthropology.uchicago.edu/about-us/history.
[122] Chumley and Harkness, "Introduction," 3.
[123] Nancy D. Munn, *The Fame of Gawa: A Symbolic Study of Value Transformation in a Massim (Papua New Guinea) Society* (Cambridge: Cambridge University Press, 1986).

Through producing these qualisigns, Munn argues, value is also produced, and as a result, so are "selves, relationships, communities, and also hierarchies and inequalities."[124]

Although Munn, Chumley, and Harkness explore these ideas in the field of semiotic anthropology, these concepts also have applications to open notations. One idea central to my analysis comes from Harkness's paper "Softer Soju in South Korea." He connects qualia such as "softness" across multiple modes of semiotic engagement related to the drinking of *soju*,[125] including fricative voice gestures (the sound made following a drink), the taste of *soju*, and gendered qualities in advertising of different brands. He designates the cross-modal perception of qualia as *qualic transitivity*.[126] In *Songs of Seoul: An Ethnography of Voice and Voicing in Christian South Korea*, Harkness considers the role of qualic transitivity in mediating the relationship between voice and emotion for *songak* singers and the larger social ideologies of modern Christian South Korea.[127] The focus on "stable," "joyful," and "clean" voices, which are quite the departure from the "rough," "husky," and "unclean" voices of the past, index the advancement of modern South Korea.[128]

In my work, qualic transitivity is mainly discussed as mediating indexical connections among notations and conceptualized musical actions. For example, in Section 3 of this text, I argue that the visual qualities of open notations play a critical role in determining their semiotic function. However, qualic transitivity does not merely describe the connection of visual and aural qualia, but more broadly indexes across many different domains. In Harkness's work, haptic qualia are often considered – the feeling of *soju* in the throat, or the sensation of singing in a strained or open manner. Certainly the haptic is relevant to the interpretation of open notations as well; for a pianist, the appearance of a notation may index the sensation of playing certain notes or chords, articulation, or even choreography.

3 Into the Wilderness: Semiotic Analysis in Practice

Redman asks performers to play a greater role in the creation of a performance through taking on a large amount of interpretive power; his works "[invite] the

---

[124] Chumley and Harkness, "Introduction," 6.
[125] *Soju* is a distilled alcoholic beverage popular in South Korea.
[126] Nicholas Harkness, "Softer Soju in South Korea," *Anthropological Theory* 13, no. 1–2 (2013), 12–30 at 26.
[127] Western classical style.
[128] Harkness, *Songs of Seoul*, 46–47.

beholder into a wilderness of interpretive self-sufficiency."[129] The metaphor of score-as-wilderness is an effective one. Wild natural spaces and open scores similarly demand an adventurous and enterprising spirit of those who seek to navigate them. In this section, I apply theory to practice in the analysis of works by Brown (Section 3.1), Redman (Section 3.2), and Asher (Section 3.3).

3.1 Pitch Content As Symbol System in Brown's *Folio* (1952–1953)

Brown's *Folio* is comprised of seven pieces, but here I consider pitch content in just two of them: *November 1952* and *December 1952*. Two questions drive my analyses: how does conventional pitch notation operate as a symbol system in Goodman's terms, and how do these two pieces from *Folio* work within or subvert this system? In *Languages of Art*, Goodman argues that notational systems are mediated by syntactic and semantic guidelines. The musical score, acting as a notational system, preserves the definitive identity of a musical work upon which all performances are measured; only through complete compliance with the score is a genuine performance of a work possible.[130] On this larger scale, Goodman considers entire scores to be units in a notation system. Scores must be unambiguously compliant with performances, and performances of a score must be unambiguously compliant with the score.[131] On a more local level, in order for scores to do the job of notating, they must be *digital symbol systems* in which elements are syntactically and semantically differentiated and disjoint.[132] Additionally, each mark must indicate only one possible symbol. For pitch material, this means that noteheads must not correlate with more than one pitch. Pitch notation must be differentiated and disjoint both syntactically and semantically. To illustrate these requirements, we can consider the standard notation system.[133]

In conventional music notation, pitch is indicated by the placement of notes on the five-line staff. Notes can be placed on any of the five lines of the staff, or on the four spaces between. I refer to the lines and spaces notes occupy on the staff as nodes. The staff can notate more than nine pitches, however. Ledger lines extend the staff by continuing the trajectory of nodes above and below its

---

[129] Redman, "Short Bio."

[130] Goodman, *Languages of Art*, 186.

[131] Goodman, *Languages of Art*, 128–130.

[132] For more on Goodman's theory of symbol systems, see "Symbol Systems" in Section 2.2.

[133] In this section, I distinguish *notes, pitches,* and *frequencies*. Notes are musical notation signs placed on the staff; they are notated. Pitches are abstract musical sounds indicated by notes (C, D, E, etc.). Frequencies are concrete hertz measurements of a pitched sound (the pitch A tuned to different frequencies can be 440 Hz, 442 Hz, 432 Hz, etc.).

five lines. Signs indicate the displacement of notated pitches by the octave, so that the sounding pitch is displaced by one octave (*8va*, or *ottava*) or two octaves (*15ma*, or *quindicesima*). Clefs are used at the beginning of each system of music to lock in the lines and spaces of the staff to signify specific pitches.[134] In keyboard music, two clefs are used, generally in pairs: treble and bass. For treble clef, the lines from bottom to top indicate pitches E, G, B, D, and F. The spaces between the five lines indicate F, A, C, and E. For bass clef, the lines from bottom to top indicate pitches G, B, D, F, and A, and the spaces indicate A, C, E, and G. Clef, staff lines, ledger lines, and octave-displacement signs are all examples of what I call *framing notations*. These signs are non-sounding elements that create a structured framework for notes.

The representation of pitch on the staff relates pitch to the vertical axis so that the higher a note is, the higher its corresponding pitch; this is called diastematic notation. Similarly, the lower a note is on the staff, the lower its corresponding pitch. However, there are some exceptions to this rule where the relation among notes on the vertical axis in the score does not accurately reflect the difference in frequency of the sounding pitches. For example, a change in clef on a single line can disrupt this rule. Consider the notation of an E in the treble clef (on the first line) followed by an A in the bass clef (on the fifth line). When notated, the second note appears to be much higher than the first (Figure 7).

However, the change in clef results in a lower-sounding pitch for the second note. For another example, consider a grand staff (two linked staves with treble and bass clef), commonly used in keyboard notation (Figure 8).

The first note is an E notated in the bass clef two ledger lines above the staff. The second note is a C notated in the treble clef one ledger line below the staff. Even though the second note is higher on the page than the first, the sounding pitch is lower. Finally, octave displacement signs such as *8va* and *15ma* easily lead to inconsistencies with the diastematic structure of the staff. Take for example the treble staff with an F on the fifth line with an *8va* sign above, followed by a G on the space above the fifth line that is *loco* (Figure 9).

Although the second note appears to be a step higher than the first on the page, the sounding pitches are nearly an octave apart. The sounding pitch for the first note is indeed higher than the second. The range of notated pitch is

---

[134] The word "system" here refers to a line of musical notation. For an economical use of space, notated music is frequently broken into systems, though there is no audible transition from one system to another. This is comparable to the breaking up of text into lines on the page, where the visual break from one line of text to another does not necessarily impact the reading of that sentence.

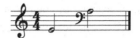

Figure 7 Diastematic exception 1

Figure 8 Diastematic exception 2

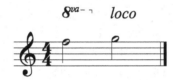

Figure 9 Diastematic exception 3

theoretically unlimited; one could extend the notation of a pitch upward or downward indefinitely by continuing to add octave displacement signs. However, there is a practical limitation to this notation as there are boundaries to what any acoustic instrument can perform. Donald Byrd cites the highest-notated and highest-sounding pitch as being G#8 (MIDI note number 116) in Salvatore Sciarrino's *Six Caprices for Violin*, no. 1 (1976), and the lowest-notated and lowest-sounding pitch as being C0 (MIDI note number 12) in Alexandre Guilmant's *Organ Sonata no. 5* in C, Op. 80 (before 1909).[135]

Despite some inconsistencies in the mapping of pitch to vertical placement on the staff, the system of framing notations locks the nodes of the staff to discrete pitches so that there is no ambiguity between the symbols and their referents. In this way, any note that appears in the third space from the bottom of the treble clef staff is a C, unless altered by an accident by way of key signature or local placement of a sharp or flat. This is what Goodman refers to as *character-indifference*;[136] this pitch notation system does not consider any difference

---

[135] Donald Byrd, "Extremes of Conventional Music Notation," Indiana University Bloomington, revised mid-October 2018. Accessed December 17, 2019. http://homes.soic.indiana.edu/don byrd/CMNExtremes.htm

[136] Goodman, *Languages of Art*, 132.

among C's notated on this line.[137] Standard notation meets Goodman's
demands for syntactic differentiation and disjoinedness. To be disjoint, each
mark must belong to no more than one symbol. In notation, each note on the
staff belongs to no more than one pitch. There are no occasions of symbolic
overlap where a note could refer to multiple pitches. To be syntactically
differentiated and finite, it must always be possible to tell to which symbol
a mark belongs. In conventional notation, it is always possible to tell to which
pitch a note belongs. The array of possible frequencies for notated pitch is
continuous in that for any two frequencies another is possible between.
However, standard notation breaks down this frequency spectrum into discrete
intervals, the smallest of which is the half step. In the Western tonal system, no
pitch is found between any two half steps, and thus the syntactical system of
pitch notation is a digital one. For example, assuming a standard tuning,
a C-sharp (C#5) would have a frequency of 554.37 Hz, while the note directly
above it, D5, would have a frequency of 587.33 Hz. While the range of possible
frequencies is continuous (555.37 or 557.4 are two possible frequencies out of
an infinite number that fall between the original two frequencies), the range
standard notation affords is composed of semantically differentiated and disjoint frequencies, and therefore not all frequencies are available for use.
Differences in tuning that may alter frequency are not accounted for in
Goodman's theory, as it is concerned with notes and pitches, not frequencies.

While syntax in pitch notation is primarily concerned with the realm of
notes, semantics in pitch notation is primarily concerned with the realm of
pitches. Standard notation also meets Goodman's requirements for semantic differentiation and disjointedness. To be semantically disjoint, each
symbol must be distinct from each other symbol in the system. In pitch
notation, this means that each pitch must be distinct from each other pitch.
For example, the pitch C is distinct from each other pitch in the system – it
is never D or E. To be semantically differentiated, it must always be
possible to tell to which mark a symbol belongs. In notation, this means
that pitches must unambiguously be connected to notes, so that the pitch
C could never indicate the note D or E.

In *November 1952* (Figure 10), pitches are represented using notes, and
durational values are represented with conventional rhythmic notations including quarter notes, eighth notes, and sixteenth notes. No meter is indicated, and
there are no bar lines or rests. Dynamic marks, which indicate volume (or the

---

[137] This argument does not take into account differences in tuning, which may have intentional and
unintentional variations. Baroque ensembles frequently tune lower than their modern counter-
parts, and pianos eventually go out of tune.

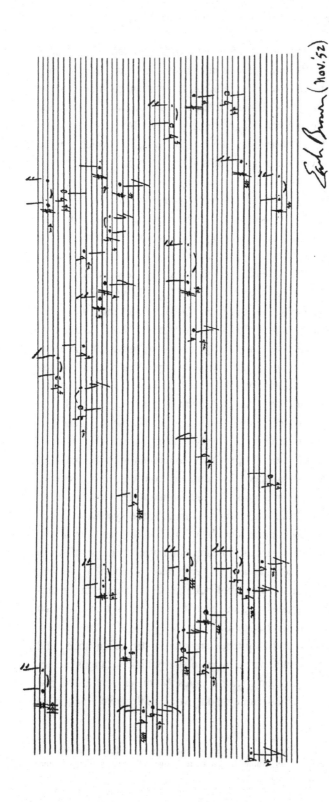

Figure 10 *November 1952* from *Folio* (1952–1953) by Earle Brown

relative "intensity" as Brown calls it), are represented by conventional symbols such as *mp*, *ff*, and *pp*.[138]

Brown's note on *November 1952* provides valuable insight into the boundaries and limits of a valid interpretation.

> The frequency range will be relative to that of each instrument performing the work.[139] To be performed in any direction from any point in the defined space for any length of time. Tempo: as fast as possible to as slow as possible ... inclusive. Attacks may be interpreted as completely separated by infinite space, collectively in blocks of any shape, or defined exactly within that space. Line and spaces may be thought of as tracks moving in either direction (horizontally at different and variable speeds) and clef signs may be considered as floating (vertically over the defined space) ... this indicates the theoretical possibility of all the attacks occurring at the same instant (and on the same frequency, for any amount of time) or any other expression of simultaneity. The defined space may be thought of as real or illusory, as a whole or in parts. Either space (vertical or horizontal) may expand, contract, or remain as it seems to be here. Vertical space will vary according to the performer's view of the floating clefs.[140]

Brown makes some contradictory claims with regard to pitch. Pitch is mapped to the vertical axis so that the higher a note is positioned on the page, the higher its corresponding pitch, and vice versa. However, the same practical range as ordinary five-line staff notation does not limit this pitch notation. Although Brown uses a fifty-line staff in *November 1952*, he writes that the frequency range of the score emulates the range of instrument on which it is performed.[141] This renders the pitch material relative, so that any note can correspond to any pitch. Although pitch corresponds to the vertical axis, it is still ambiguously notated, as there are no clefs. If Brown had included a single clef on his fifty-line staff, the pitch content of his score would have been tethered to discrete pitches, and the intervallic relationships in his notation would be preserved in its identity as a digital symbol system. Instead, he instructs the performer to consider clefs "floating (vertically over the defined space)," so that the vertical axis for pitch can expand and contract freely.[142] He goes so far as to suggest that given this, the entire piece, with all its variations in vertical note placement, could be played on a single pitch.

The pitch notation in *November 1952* does not meet Goodman's notational requirements for syntax. Because there is no clef, Brown's notation is not disjoint,

---

[138] Brown, "Prefatory Note."

[139] Brown refers to the "frequency range" of instruments. I use "pitch" to describe sounding diatonic pitches.

[140] Brown, "Prefatory Note."

[141] Brown, "Prefatory Note."

[142] Brown, "Prefatory Note."

as a note can indicate a multitude of different pitches. A note on the bottom line of the staff can indicate any pitch. Perhaps on the keyboard, this would be the lowest note (A0) as Brown wrote that the vertical dimension of the staff should correspond to the range of the instrument. Or perhaps the performer imagines a treble clef positioned just before this note, so that it denotes an E just above middle C (E4). Without a clef to lock in the nodes of the staff to discrete pitches, this note does not correspond to any pitch in particular. Similarly, it is not possible to tell to which pitch any single note belongs, so it is not syntactically differentiated and finite.

This system is semantically disjoint in that nothing in the notation alters the field of referents, in this case pitch classes. This is the only one of Goodman's notational requirements with which *November 1952* complies. Brown's instructions do not challenge conventional pitch content resolution. Even though performers are given absolute freedom regarding harmonic content, this system can still be said to have a pitch class resolution at the half step, the smallest available interval. Despite the mobility of specific notes, the pitch content afforded by the symbol system remains the same. In other words, because *November 1952* still uses a staff to frame its pitches, it does not imply that the performer should seek out frequencies outside of the diatonic pitch set. The nodes of the staff signify diatonic pitches, albeit indeterminately and openly. Although this notation is semantically disjoint, it is not semantically differentiated. It is not always possible to tell to which note a pitch belongs, as the connection between pitch and nodes of the staff is unregulated. If we consider the pitch E (or more specifically E4, the one just above middle C), there is no single node on the fifty-line staff in *November 1952* to signify this pitch.

December 1952 can be conceptualized in three dimensions (vertical, horizontal, and time) or four dimensions (vertical, horizontal, depth, and time).[143] I consider a three-dimensional orientation of the score. The influence of Calder and Pollock is obvious in this piece, as Brown emphasizes the mobility of his notations by stating that the score may be "performed from any of the four rotational positions in any sequence" so that there are four possible orientations.[144] He notes that for a performance that considers three dimensions, "the thickness of the event may indicate relative intensity and/or clusters"[145] (Figure 11).

The performance instructions included in the prefatory note are somewhat cryptic with regard to pitch, but an interview with Brown provides insight into one performance he conducted of the score in Darmstadt in 1964.[146] In this interview, Brown says that he instructed the performers of the Darmstadt

---

[143] Brown, "On December 1952," 4–5.

[144] Brown, "Prefatory Note."

[145] Brown, "Prefatory Note."

[146] Brown, "On December 1952," 9.

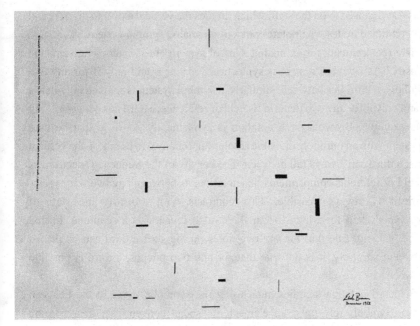

Figure 11 *December 1952* from *Folio* (1952–1953) by Earle Brown
A *Folio* AND FOUR SYSTEMS by Earle Brown Copyright © 1961 (Renewed) by
Associated Music Publishers, Inc. (BMI) International Copyright Secured. All Rights
Reserved. Reprinted by Permission

orchestra to consider pitch as related to the vertical placement of events. More
broadly, he asks performers to align visual parameters of the score (vertical axis,
horizontal axis, and imagined depth of view) with musical parameters such as
pitch, duration, and intensity.[147] Like *November 1952*, the range of pitch in
December 1952 is instrument-specific. If it were performed on the piano, its
range would span the lowest note to the highest note on the instrument;
similarly, assuming an interpretation that aligns the vertical axis of the score
with pitch, the highest point of the score would represent the highest possible
pitch on the instrument used in performance, and the lowest point on the vertical
dimension would represent the lowest possible pitch on the instrument. Yet
November and *December* differ in their pitch systems. Although Brown uses an
unusual fifty-line staff in *November*, his notation does not account for any
resolution smaller than a semitone. In *December*, by contrast, no such division
of the frequency spectrum is used. By placing notation elements on a continuous

---

[147] Brown, "Prefatory Note."

axis – as opposed to on the staff, which divides the vertical axis into discrete and differentiated nodes – he notates pitch as an analog symbol system.

The requirements for an analog symbol system are syntactic and semantic density.[148] A symbol system is syntactically dense if and only if for any two symbols, a third lies between; similarly, a symbol system is semantically dense if and only if for any two items in its field of reference, a third lies between.[149] In this example, Brown's pitch notation is syntactically dense in that he uses a system with an infinitely divisible resolution; for any two points on the vertical axis, a third can always fall between. The density of the frequency spectrum as a field of referents complements this notation, as between any two frequencies a third is always possible. This contrasts with the fifty-line staff of *November 1952* for which the smallest pitch division is a semitone. In that piece, it is not true that for any two notes on the staff a third can be placed between; similarly, it is not true that for any two pitches, a third is possible between.

Standard notation signifies pitch using the symbolic mode in the Peircean sense. Symbols rely upon an element of "social convention"; their specific content is only accessible to someone who knows the code.[150] In other words, nothing about a note located on the bottom line of a treble staff has anything inherently "E" about it. Instead, this knowledge requires an understanding of the conventions related to this system of notation. Standard pitch notation operates as a system because it meets Goodman's syntactic and semantic requirements for notation. It relies upon the symbolic mode of signification; there is no room for ambiguity in either case. While Goodman's theory does not account for ambiguity in notation, as he considers any score that fails to meet his requirements non-notational, Peirce's theory does. The way forward with analysis is to consider the semiotic implications of pitch content used in these two pieces – namely, if these systems are non-notational according to Goodman, and nonsymbolic in the Peircean sense, what other modes of signification do they employ?

Elements of mobility, while at first most apparent in the notations of *December 1952*, are also an integral part of *November 1952*. Without clef(s) to anchor the nodes of the staff to discrete pitches, Brown effectively denies the performer a symbolic reading of pitch. That said, Peirce's theory emphasizes the complexity of signification, including the hierarchical nesting of multiple modes of signification.[151] The axis orientation of pitch affords the performer indexical information, in which signs related to pitch are mediated by "some

[148] Goodman, *Languages of Art*, 180.
[149] Goodman, *Languages of Art*, 160.
[150] Merrell, "Charles Sanders Peirce's Concept of the Sign," 31.
[151] Parmentier, *Signs in Society*, 6.

actual or physical or imagined connection" to their objects.[152] In music notation, axis orientation aligns a musical parameter with a visual parameter. In this case, the height of the note on the staff corresponds to pitch as related to the range of the instrument. A performer could easily infer the relative pitch associated with a note by considering its placement on the vertical axis as indexically related to the range of their instrument.

Brown's instructions indicate that the performer should imagine clefs superimposed on the staff. A performer who imagines them in a singular position would end up with a "fixed-pitch" reading of the entire piece. If the same performer imagined the staves fixed in three different sequential positions, three different sets of pitches result. Only if the performer imagines a clef positioned in front of every note would all ties between the vertical axis and corresponding pitch be severed. *November 1952* flirts with the destruction of the vertical pitch axis without fully committing to its demise. The fifty-line staff takes on a monolithic quality, in which notes appear to float over an array of potential pitches. Relationships among pitches are indexically related to their vertical distance from one another on the page so that qualities of relative interval become prescient information. Vertical proximity becomes another quality indicative of pitch, so that notes that are close together on the vertical axis indicate relatively close pitches. "Imagining" clefs disrupts this indexical relationship in the same way that a clef change in standard notation disrupts the vertical relationship among notes and pitches. Real or imagined, clefs symbolically lock pitch to the nodes of the staff. A change in clef disregards the indexical relationship between verticality on the page and the range of indicated pitches.

In *December 1952*, pitch is aligned to an axis, but not necessarily the vertical axis as Brown leaves this variable open to the performer. Range is again instrument-specific. One key element that differentiates *December 1952* from *November 1952* is that it utilizes an analog symbol system to inscribe its marks. In an interview with Brown, he briefly mentions David Tudor's performance of *Four Systems* (1954), another piece of Brown's that uses lines to approximate pitch on the vertical axis.

> His approach was not at all improvisational. He used rulers and calipers and various things in order to find exactly vertically what pitches were involved and the durations. In other words, he transcribed the graphics of Four Systems into a kind of standard notation ... but this didn't interest me. I could have taken any one of these scores and made a fixed, final version – that was not my point, although I don't at all criticize David's doing it that way.[153]

---

[152] Merrell, "Charles Sanders Peirce's Concept of the Sign," 31.

[153] Brown, "On December 1952," 8–9.

Theoretically a performer could, like Tudor, measure the distance from the bottom to the top of the page, divide it into eighty-eight sections to correspond with the number of keys on a piano, and derive pitches for the lines based on this analysis. Yet the use of an analog symbol system complicates matters for the pianist, and this type of realization would be no more accurate to the score than one that is approximated without measurement. Unlike a string instrument, for example, the piano cannot accommodate intervals smaller than the semitone; in this respect, the piano necessitates a digital production of pitch material. A glissando performed on the violin is a continuous and analog translation of pitch material; on the piano, it is not. If through measuring the distance between points on the vertical axis the performer derives frequencies between the keys on the piano, the only option is to approximate to the nearest pitch. The most accurate representation of this material as mapped on an axis would be with numerals, so that a reading could be as close to the visual analog as possible – yet unless this is performed by a computer, this type of reading is not possible. Such a reading would utilize the iconic mode of signification, as the dimension of height on the page precisely indicates the referenced frequencies of sound.

Frequently, interpretations like Tudor's are absorbed into the ongoing performance practice of a piece; they contribute new layers to the entextualization of the score. Documents outside of the score including recordings, interviews, or archived performance scores are indicators of a singular encounter with a score that often contribute to a conventionalization of interpretation. In Peircean terms, Tudor's interpretation of the score is a sinsign, a singular interpretation of the marks on the score; the conventionalization of his performance, for example his approach to measuring the distance among the marks and calculating precise values for pitch, would render the sinsigns legisigns, for which rules and guidelines exist that extend past the singular performance. Tudor's performance is uniquely entextualized in the documentation that surrounds it, which is mediated by a number of social relationships: Brown's position of power as the composer of the work, the authority of the interview, and Tudor's position as the performer who premiered the work. Calling into question notable moments of discourse such as this in the life of a score-as-text reconnects the interpreter to the full array of possibilities the notations afford. While I position the relationship between notations in *December 1952* and conceptualized sound as indexical (by way of perceived qualities) and Tudor considered them iconic (by way of measured physical properties), there is also a case to be made for reading these notations as indexical icons. Indexical icons are thought to have a likeness to their objects by a causal relationship and resemblance. There is an element of naturalization at work that makes the indexical icon seem obvious or inevitable. In the case of *December 1952*, an interpretation that treats the horizontal axis as time and the vertical axis as pitch parallels the treatment of axes in conventional notation; this orientation relates musical and spatial parameters as indexical icons. It indexes the familiar or natural orientation of conventional notation while iconically resembling it. However, Brown's instructions allow the performer to freely assign parameters so that the indexical-iconic orientation is but one option among many.

Goodman's theory allows us to examine the systems of representation at work in this score more abstractly. At first, there seems to be some friction in creating a digital reading of an analog symbol system, in the way that approximating points in a full frequency spectrum on the limited pitches of a piano does. After all, Goodman reminds us that "a system of this kind is the very antithesis of a notational system."[154] However, this is exactly the type of revision to Goodman's theory that Kulvicki pursues. He posits that although the readings utilize an analog symbol system, we never perceive them as such in our interactions.[155] The scale accompanying a mercury thermometer offers an approximate, but accurate enough scale for our practical needs. Functionally, the analog notation of *December 1952* is similar: an interpretation of pitch does not need to take into account the intricacies of the marks as analog, but rather the relationships among them. An alternative reading of pitch in *December 1952* might focus on qualities that relate the horizontal and vertical lines. Notational qualities related to proximity (closeness and distance) and density (thickness and thinness) can be read as indexical indicators of qualities related to pitch, where proximity on the vertical axis correlates to proximity of pitch, and density correlates to density of pitches. This move toward the indexical, toward the reading of qualities over a structural mapping of analog pitch content, is more in line with Brown's conception of *December 1952* as a kinetic notation.

November 1952 and *December 1952* are two works by Brown written in open notation. However an analysis of pitch notation systems reveals that they integrate openness and ambiguity in different ways on a structural level. Neither piece meets the standards of notation specified by Goodman; *November 1952* is not syntactically disjoint and differentiated, and, although it is semantically disjoint, it is not semantically differentiated. The only component in *November 1952* that meets Goodman's requirements for a notational system is semantic disjointedness. In other words, Brown's notation does not challenge the field of referenced pitches. This score denies the performer a symbolic reading through its destabilization of pitch notation. Instead,

---

[154] Goodman, *Languages of Art*, 160.
[155] Kulvicki, "Analog Representation and the Parts Principle," 165–180.

performers are encouraged to engage with an indexical reading that openly and flexibly relates pitch to vertical position.

December 1952, as conceptualized in three dimensions, relates pitch to an axis in the score. This analog symbol system is syntactically and semantically dense, as between any two points on the pitch axis another is possible, and between any two referenced frequencies another is possible. *December 1952* violates all four of Goodman's notational requirements, as even its field of referents (frequency) is smooth. An iconic reading of this piece is not possible on the piano, as the "rounding" of frequencies to their closest corresponding diatonic pitches would not preserve the isomorphic relationship of frequency to positions on the notated axis. In this way, there is friction between the symbols as an analog system and an interpretation that estimates. In opposition to this, Kulvicki argues that many analog symbol systems are read more generally. An indexical reading of *December 1952* that estimates pitch is still in line with the analogicity of the score.

In crafting an indexical reading of *November 1952* and *December 1952*, performers can consider a few things. First, when rehearsing or studying these works, the performer should decide what is predetermined and what is left open for performance. In *November 1952*, Brown leaves it to the performer to "imagine clefs" superimposed over the score. If the performer prepares an interpretation of this piece by placing clefs and creating a fully determinate score, they essentially re-notate the score as a closed work. Certainly the work in the abstract still allows for any number of different re-notations, but in perform-ance, the indexical and open nature of the work is subverted and replaced by a symbolic score. Any performance of this work is only a single frame of the work in motion, not unlike a photograph of a Calder mobile as opposed to the mobile itself; however with re-notating, the mobility and openness of the work is less immediate and salient for the performer. The immediacy, openness, and movement of the work are dulled.

Similarly, if a performer were to carefully measure and determine the closest approximate pitch in *December 1952* as Tudor did, they would end up with a re-notated score, a single outcome of an open and flexible work. Yet again, the openness of the work is disregarded in performance and the performer's engagement with the score is not indexical but symbolic. Perhaps the value of working with the original score is more obvious here, as re-notating *December 1952* for performance on the piano is necessarily flawed; since the piano approximates the frequency spectrum at the level of the semitone, the analog nature of the pitch notation must be approximated. Re-notating this work for performance inevitably produces an estimation rather than a realization. A reading that more immediately relies upon an indexical reading of pitch carries with it the flexible and mobile nature of the work to the performer's engagement with the score.

An indexical interpretation of *November 1952* would emphasize a reading of proximity in relation to the staff as well as among the notes. The performer may spontaneously imagine clefs superimposed on the staff in performance. They may even rely upon a more intuitive reading of the notation by following the feelings or sensations associated with each note. For example, a note two spaces from the top of the fifty-line staff may signify "E-ness," as the second space from the top of the bass staff is E. Abstract spatial qualities of notes may carry over from experience with conventional notations. If the following note were two spaces below, the proximity of the two notes may read as being a fifth apart. In other words, there may be "fifth-ness" about the proximity of the notes. *December 1952* is different in that the scale of pitch remains the same for the entire piece. The range of pitch is based on the range of the instrument on which it is played. A performer may freely estimate pitch based on this range, so that a line halfway up the page would be halfway up the keyboard; a line roughly one-eighth from the top of the page would be one-eighth from the top of the keyboard. This type of meaning making is fully embraced by both the score and Brown's instructions.

There may be more of a temptation to re-notate Brown's works because of their clear use of symbol systems. Brown outlines specific decisions for the performer to make, such as aligning certain musical parameters to clear visual parameters in the score. By following his rules and guidelines, the performer can create a fully determinate interpretation by making only a few decisions.

3.2 *Erasure, Oversaturation*, and *Extension* in Redman's *Book* (2006)

In Section 1.2, I gave an overview of Redman's aesthetics and approach to ambiguity. To illuminate what is ambiguous about his notations, I consider the notations from a single page of *Book* (2006) (Figure 12). I show that Redman utilizes three primary compositional strategies to integrate ambiguity into this score: erasure, oversaturation, and extension. I employ semiotics to show in particular how Redman's notations emphasize the indexical mode of significa-tion, and that their openness engenders creative acts in performance.

One way Redman fosters ambiguity is through *erasure*, or the intentional absence of certain notation elements. In *Book*, framing notations – on-sounding notation signs that assist in designating harmonic and rhythmic content – are absent to varying degrees. Some examples of harmonic framing

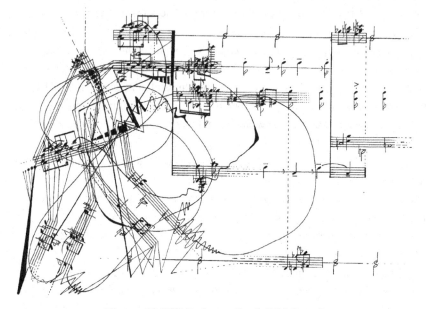

Figure 12 Will Redman. *Book* (2006), p. 3

signs include staff lines and clef. The staff supplies a frame onto which notes
can be placed, with its lines and spaces acting as nodes that signify pitch.
Clefs orient the nodes of the staff around discrete pitches; on a staff with
a treble clef, the pitch indicated by the bottom line is E, and for a staff with
a bass clef, the pitch indicated by the bottom line is G. Key signatures (the
sharps and flats indicated at the beginning of each line of music) provide
global information for pitch alteration and, in tonal music, the major or minor
key; an F-sharp in the key signature indicates that any note on an F node of
the staff becomes an F-sharp. Rhythmic framing signs include meter and time
signature, bar lines, and beams. Like harmonic framing notations, this material provides a framework for designating rhythmic content, but is itself tacit.
Time signatures provide global information relating to the meter of the piece.
Vertical bar lines parse the staff into horizontal segments of regulated time, as
implied by the meter. Note beams provide local information relating to
duration. With the absence of time signature or meter (as would be reinforced
by regular bar lines), the sense of pulse or rhythm is indistinct. In turn, the
performer has greater control over the hierarchical relationship between
sound events.

Aside from framing notations, other non-sounding signs include
dynamics, character markings, and articulation markings, among others.

Figure 13 Redman, *Book* (2006), p. 3 excerpt

Dynamic signs indicate relative intensity or volume, character markings are textual indicators of tone and character, and articulation markings indicate alterations to the duration and intensity of specific notes. These signs are not part of larger networks, but act independently. Their absence does not render anything unreadable or unplayable; no larger systems depend on them. With harmonic and rhythmic framing notations, one absent element renders the content ambiguous. Redman engages with erasure of framing notations in a number of different ways. Figure 13 shows a group of noteheads with accidentals and beams on a five-line staff.

The five-line staff supplies some framing information, but without a clef it is not discrete. If a treble clef were superimposed in front of this passage, the first note would signify a G-flat; if a bass clef were superimposed in front, the first note would signify a B-flat. But with no clef present, the notation cannot determine pitch with any specificity. The symbolic function of the harmonic content is denied. Even though this passage does not convey distinct pitch content, it does signify pitch information in a more general way. For example, the relative contour of the passage remains the same whether or not a clef is present. In this way, it is clear that the first note gives way to a dyad (two-note chord) in which the top note is a third higher. A single note a third lower than the lower note of the dyad follows. The intervallic content of this passage, while not as discrete as if a clef were present, is still present is a more indexical way. The verticality of the noteheads on the page points to the verticality of pitch content as conceptualized by the performer. This reading preserves a mapping of pitch to the vertical axis, but without specifying what each node symbolizes in conceptual space. It takes knowledge of clef and staff to read specific notes on a fully notated score (symbolic function), but someone without this knowledge can see the relative contour of markings on a page (indexical function). Figure 14, similarly, is notated without a clef. However, read from left to right it also conveys a disappearing staff.

What begins as a five-line staff on the left gradually fades to blank space. Solid lines turn dotted before disappearing completely, all at different rates.

Figure 14 Redman, *Book* (2006), p. 3 excerpt

Figure 15 Redman, *Book* (2006), p. 3 excerpt

While it could be argued that the staff lines afford opportunity for sounding (discussed further in the section on extension), this is a more metaphorical expression of erasure: the lines of the staff, so central to harmonic framing information, vanish. In Figure 15, the five-line staff is truncated and reduced to a single line. By the end of this short excerpt, the single line turns dashed, then dotted, and then it disappears entirely.

This passage is significant as a variation on Figures 13 and 14. In addition to lacking a clef, four out of five staff lines are absent. This renders the staff even more ambiguous, as clear nodes of the staff used to measure interval are not provided. On its own, the solitary line could signify any pitch. When reading the relative interval of the notes surrounding this line, a level of exactness is further removed. In this example, the dyads are clearly a third apart. But notes that are positioned further apart may be less clear. In this way, the quality of relative interval conveyed by this material is less measured. Going one step further, the staff is completely absent in Figure 16, leaving the notes free-floating in the blank space of the page.

Without any staff lines present, what harmonic material do these notes afford? These notes could be freely interpreted, since they have no frame of reference. Despite the absence of the staff, we can still posit meaningful relationships among the notes. Each dyad in Figure 16 is spaced approximately a fifth or sixth apart, a quality apparent to anyone with experience reading music. They most certainly are not an octave apart, and they are not in unison. Both dyads are the same interval, so their proximity also expresses an element of repetition. This notation still conveys intervallic qualities, albeit even more ambiguously than the single staff line shown in Figure 15.

Figure 16 Redman, *Book* (2006), p. 3 excerpt

Figure 17 Redman, *Book* (2006), p. 3 excerpt

Redman also employs *oversaturation*, in which notations are layered over one another so that their conventional affordances are obscured. In these cases, the noteheads to varying degrees form a tangled mass, where the number of noteheads is indistinct and their placement on the staff is unclear. In Figure 17, some notes are distinct while others are not.

The three notes on the left side of the figure are completely disjoint, whereas the chord in the middle is muddled. It is unclear how many notes are in this chord, what accidentals (sharps, flats, and naturals) are present, and to which notes they apply. Articulation markings such as staccato are clear for the leftmost notes of the excerpt, but are lost in the denser area; the alignment of noteheads and beams is similarly ambiguous. Generally, noteheads iconically signify the number of sounding pitches. In the performance of a melody with sixteen notes, one expects to hear sixteen sounding pitches. Of course there are exceptions; tied notes extend the duration of a previous attack without adding an additional one, so that two notes tied together sound like a single pitch. Tied notes arise out of the need to notate a duration that extends over a bar line, or to clarify durations in relation to the meter. The mass of notes in the middle of Figure 17 cannot iconically signify the number of pitches to be played, because that information is ambiguous. Instead, it affords other musical qualities relating to density, intervallic spread, and duration. In terms of density, this cluster of notes appears to have somewhere between five and six noteheads spread out roughly in thirds. The chord is top-heavy, as it is denser at the top than the bottom. Rhythmically, this chord has all filled-in notes with stems connecting to

Figure 18 Redman, *Book* (2006), p. 3 excerpt

Figure 19 Redman, *Book* (2006), p. 3 excerpt

the sixteenth note beam on the bottom, an eighth flag on the top, and a quarter note stem on the left side. These notes afford several different durations, though it is not clear which notes among them should have the longer durations. Finally, although the accidentals are indistinct, several of them are definitely natural signs, which cancel a sharp or flat; if performed on the piano, this chord affords a white-note quality, as natural pitches are always white keys. Figure 18 illustrates oversaturation much in the same way as Figure 17.

Certain notes and their related markings are distinct while others are muddled by oversaturation. However, Figure 18 is denser than Figure 17. The quality of density is not restricted to the interpretation of isolated chords, but is afforded on a larger scale by phrases and passages. Figure 19 exemplifies oversaturation in a different way. There is hardly any overlap among the relatively sparse noteheads, yet the horizontal displacement of notes gives the impression of multiple layers of notation.

Even though this passage consists mainly of eighth and quarter notes, and there is no implication of measured polyrhythm, the spacing of the notes affords the quality of disjointedness. This passage is oversaturated with metrical information. Figure 19 echoes elements of spatial notation, an alternative approach to notating the relation of sound events to time. In spatial notation, the space on the page of the score is isomorphically representative of the passage of time. In other words, there is a direct correlation between space and time, so that one unit of space on the page, such as an inch, is equal to one unit of time, such as five seconds. This practice contrasts with conventional notation, in which the

Figure 20 Redman, *Book* (2006), p. 3 excerpt

physical length of measures on the page varies depending on how much material is contained within each measure.

Some of the more provocative and eye-catching notations in *Book* relate to the lines of the staff. In conventionally notated pieces, the staff generally occupies a space in the background – a blank staff parallels the blank canvas, a neutral foundation. In *Book*, staff lines take on new characteristics. Lines rarely run in parallel groups of five, and instead have distinct and diverse qualities to them: wavy, jagged, disappearing, emerging, and bold. Redman *extends* these framing signs' ordinary function in conventional notation by giving them provocative qualities. And since Redman leaves interpretation fully to the discretion of the performer, these signs most certainly afford sounds of their own. We have already seen something similar to Figure 20 in Figure 14; staff lines lose their solid quality, become dotted or dashed, and eventually disappear.

This notation poses an interesting dilemma to the performer: if such a notation should induce sound, do staff lines also sound when they are performing their normative framing function? Alternatively, does the notational role of the lines change depending upon context, sometimes playing the part of the silent frame, and other times a dynamic signifier of sound? We cannot answer this question, as Redman gives no guidance for how these notations should be interpreted. Instead, I consider new possible meanings that extend the role of the staff lines to a sounding one.

The possibilities for interpreting these lines are vast. The quality of density as it relates to pitch in Figures 17 and 18 relies upon the notion that noteheads signify pitch and that pitch is organized from low to high on a vertical axis. The visual qualities of Figure 20, however, are not anchored to any quality or musical parameter in particular. The performer may opt to preserve the naturalized practice of considering pitch a function of the vertical axis and time a function of the horizontal axis. In this way, perhaps this notation conveys a five-note chord (signified by the vertical position of the five lines) sustained once for a long duration and then six times with a short duration (signified by the horizontal length of the lines). In Figure 21, staff lines break out of their five-line orientation and oscillate like sine waves. Reading from left to right, the waves gradually thin until just a couple remain.

Figure 21 Redman, *Book* (2006), p. 3 excerpt

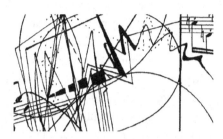

Figure 22 Redman, *Book* (2006), p. 3 excerpt

Amidst the waves, one staff line continues the trajectory of the initial line, dotted instead of solid. The excerpt shown in Figure 22 exemplifies chaos and disjointedness.

The tangle of lines are curvy, jagged, blocky, dotted, dashed, angular, bolded, and overlapping. In performance, the quality of disorder can be mirrored by rapidly switching among the lines. There is a difference in parsing out each line individually, moving among them intuitively and spontaneously, and reading in a single motion from left to right. Each would result in a different sound, the first clean and isolated, the later two chaotic.

Through erasure and oversaturation, Redman recontextualizes conventional notations and renders them ambiguous through strategic *downshifting*. Peirce conceived of downshifting as the "tendency of certain of the [sign] classes to be systematically apperceived by their interpretants as being lower-ranking signs."[156] While this is not a case relating to systematic perception but rather intentional action on the part of the composer, downshifting remains a suitable description of the effect. When the symbolic meanings of conventional notations are stripped away through the erasure of framing notations, the performer is left to infer musical meaning from the visual qualities of the marks. Rather than reading a discrete note made possible by the placement of a notehead on a specific node of the staff, the performer might read in terms of proximity to

---

[156] Parmentier, *Signs in Society*, 18.

other notes. The quality of relative intervalness might be inferred from the relative distance between noteheads in a chord on the page. In the case of oversaturation, the symbolic specificity of individual noteheads and accidentals is replaced with qualities of relative density of pitch content. The isomorphic relationship between the number of noteheads and the number of sounding pitches, an iconic relationship of sign and object, is obscured. Instead, the density of pitch content, an indexical relationship, is emphasized. For notations that Redman extends beyond their conventional symbolic affordances – such as his highly varied treatments of staff lines – there are no symbolic conventions to rely upon.

With erasure, oversaturation, and extension, Redman effectively emphasizes the indexical mode of signification by way of qualia. Specific and subjective, qualia are "experiences of sensuous qualities (such as colors, textures, sounds, and smells) and feelings (such as satiety, anxiety, proximity, and otherness)."[157] The connection between visual qualities of the notations on the page with musical qualities of sound as conceived of by the performer is mediated by *qualic transitivity*, which indicates the cross-modal perception of qualia.[158] In *Book*, the jaggedness of a staff line and the jaggedness of a melody are instances of qualia as perceived and conceived of by the performer. Through qualic transitivity, the performer draws connections between visual qualia in the score and qualia of conceptualized musical actions. In this way, indexical notations convey meaning to performers so that, for example, the "roundness" of an abstracted line notation parallels the "roundness" of a musical timbre, phrase structure, or sound envelope.

Book maintains its status as a score, a musical work, despite its openness. While it might not be apparent to a listener that two performances of *Book* are interpretations of the same score, the resulting sounds relate by way of a musical or notational "genetics."[159] The notation in *Book* is not randomly conceived, but rather strategically employed to provoke the performer into acts of discovery, improvisation, and innovation. Redman utilizes erasure, oversaturation, and extension, a trio of compositional strategies that recontextualize and obfuscate the symbolic function of conventional signs by placing them into new contexts. Semiotic analysis shows that these notations emphasize the indexical mode of signification, asking the performer to draw parallels between qualia of visually perceived marks on the page and qualia of conceptualized musical actions, as

---

[157] Chumley and Harkness, "Introduction," 3.

[158] Harkness, "Softer Soju in South Korea," 26.

[159] Redman's notion of a musical genetics is evinced by a syntactical design that exists at the crossroads of *grammar* and *pattern*, an expression of double syntax developed by David Lidov in *Elements of Semiotics*. This topic is explored in detail in Section 3.3.

mediated by qualic transitivity. Redman asks performers to play a greater role in the creation of a performance through taking on a large amount of interpretive power; these works "[invite] the beholder into a wilderness of interpretive self-sufficiency."[160] Thus *Book* is a kind of wilderness, a conflation and expansion of conventional notation elements. The performer, lacking the contextual completeness of these familiar signs, must openly conceptualize and realize their musical concepts.

3.3 Double Syntax: *Grammar* and *Pattern* in Asher's *TRAPPIST-1* (2017)

In Section 1.1, I noted that *December 1952* has become something of an emblem of the open score; the one-page work has come to signify an entire aesthetic of contemporary composition. A large number of performers and scholars have contributed interpretations and commentary on the score. With *TRAPPIST-1*, I am, as of now, the sole performer of this work. There is nothing emblematic about *TRAPPIST-1*, and yet its newness offers an equally valuable opportunity to build the foundation for a performance record and to offer insight into the creative process without appealing to a body of secondary texts.

Asher considers pitch and time as functions of the vertical and horizontal axes respectively, which presents the opportunity to consider what symbol systems are at work in the pitch and time notation.[161] Asher's notations are analog in that they are semantically and syntactically dense with respect to pitch and time. A purely iconic performance of *TRAPPIST-1* would demand an isomorphic resemblance between frequency-in-time and the vertical and horizontal placement of marks in the score. A performance of this type is possible with the accuracy of a computer program, but is impossible to achieve with a human performer. By using software that generates sound by reading the precise location of marks on the axes of the page, a wholly isomorphic resemblance can be achieved. While a human performer can approximate these relationships, approximation is not isomorphism. This holds true for conventionally notated music as well; the performance of a classical piece is both intentionally and unintentionally infused with expressive and inevitable alterations to timing. A tempo indication does not dictate an isomorphism between meter and time, just as discrete rhythms should not resemble a MIDI recording. Furthermore, an isomorphic reading of *TRAPPIST-1* is even less possible because of the disjoint representation of the frequency spectrum as diatonic pitches. On the keyboard,

---

[160] Redman, "Short Bio."

[161] This clear syntactical instruction contrasts with Redman's framing of *Book* as "decidedly unsystematic," with virtually no instruction or global parameters for interpretation to the performer.

the frequency range is sampled at eighty-eight points, and cannot account for frequencies between. An accurate performance of an analog score is impossible to realize on the piano. However, an isomorphic or analog performance of *TRAPPIST-1* is not Asher's intention. The mapping of pitch to the vertical axis is meant to be relative, not exact, and the mapping of time to the horizontal axis is similarly general. The flexibility of *TRAPPIST-1* is not unique to open scores. Elements such as pitch and rhythm meet Goodman's requirements of notation in that they are syntactically and semantically differentiated and disjoint, but other elements such as dynamics, character markings, and articulation markings do not. In *TRAPPIST-1*, it is easy to see relative pitch contour by virtue of the height of the notations on the page; yet on a smaller scale, a flexibility remains that allows for a nuanced interpretation of pitch. Dynamic markings parallel this relativeness, as within the bounds of dynamic marks there is room for individually shaping levels of intensity. Even within a single phrase marked *mf*, there are countless shadings of volume; perhaps the melody is voiced louder, the bass is played quieter to compensate for the resonance of the register, and the melody itself has peaks and valleys to give it a shape. Asher's symbol system may be analog, but it is not intended to be isomorphic.

In *December 1952*, Brown also uses analog symbol systems to notate pitch and time. However, Brown's notations more closely resemble a kind of schematic, where every dimension of the marks corresponds to a specific musical parameter (despite these connections being left open to the performer to assign). *TRAPPIST-1* instead situates graphics that are more abstract and less schematized onto an analog framework. While Brown's notations do not require the performer to engage with any qualities outside of the dimensions of the lines, Asher's notations require a deeper reading of and reliance upon qualia. Her notations are abstract in that they do not reference the lexicon of standard notations. Unlike Redman's *Book*, which places elements such as staff lines and conventional pitch and rhythmic markings into new contexts, Asher's piece uses entirely original notation. Using Asher's analog-yet-flexible organization of pitch and time on the vertical and horizontal axes, respectively, coupled with a focus on the qualia of the notations, we can construct an interpretation of this material by way of qualic transitivity (Figure 23).

There are two main types of material in Figure 23: low material that spans the entire page, and sparse patches of material dotted above. The low material is foggy, dense, and medium-dark, and maintains a similar consistency across the page despite some slight variations in density. These descriptors are my own; interpretation of the score begins here, before musical sound comes into play. The transcription of qualia from visual notations to other domains (words,

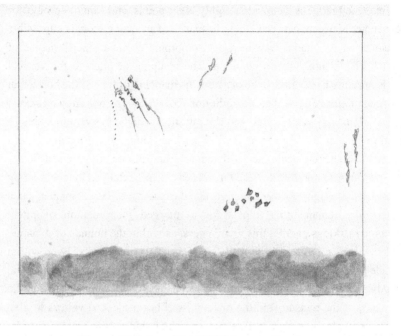

Figure 23 Asher, *TRAPPIST-1*, mov. *f*, p. 2.

sensations, feelings) is an act of interpretation. It is entirely possible to move
from the visual to the aural without a middle stage of transcription, but it is
a necessary part of writing about and describing the process. Additionally, the
transcription of visual qualia to text is helpful for communicating among
collaborators. Textual descriptors are accessible in a way that other experiences
or sensations of qualia are not. Because of its low placement on the vertical axis,
this material should make use of the lowest register on the piano. I achieved
a foggy quality to the sound by holding the sustain pedal down while lightly
patting the bass strings with the palm of my hand. This technique can easily
build up sound, so a light touch is required to maintain a consistent sound.
I avoided any sharp attacks to further emphasize the blurred quality of the
notation.

The rest of the notation on this page can be divided into three types. First,
there is a cascading arc of small dots. There are three patches of squiggly lines
with slight shading, and there is one area of diamond-shaped, shaded signs. In
relation to the large cloud of material at the bottom of the page, these notations
are small, punctuated, and contained. For the cascading dots, I used my fingernail to pluck a number of strings. I used a light touch to ensure a short decay of
sound, and used descending pitches to parallel the descending vertical

placement of the dots on the page. For the squiggly, shaded material, I used the tips of my fingers (instead of the nails) on the strings. I achieved the squiggle quality by using multiple fingers at once, which contrast with the clarity of the fingernail technique used on the cascading dot material. I approximated the range, duration, and direction of the gestures by locating them within the pitch-time axes on the page. Finally, for the diamond material, I created a hollow and slightly more resonant sound by performing muted tones in a lower register on the piano. I used one hand to mute the strings and the other hand to play the corresponding keys on the piano. The larger shape of the diamond notation encourages a larger sound, and the thickness indicates a more substantial resonance. The gray shading parallels the grayness of the foggy notation that stretches across the bottom of the page; I achieved a dull sound (rather than a sharp attack) by muting the strings.

Lidov's division of syntax into *grammar* and *pattern* is useful for parsing out how performers mediate between the score and their interpretation. These terms capture two sides of "double syntax," an approach to syntactical structures that continues the work of Jakobson, Chomsky, and Ruwet. Specifically, Lidov argues that his approach to syntax "rectifies" or "clarifies" that of Jakobson, with regard to reconciling large-scale and localized syntax.[162] "A grammar is a set of rules governing abstract categories[163] (such as 'noun' in language or 'diagonals' in chess) and combinations of their elements, and the grammar of a text can refer to the structure it exhibits as an example fitting those rules."[164] Pattern, in contrast, "is a structure that can be discovered in one text in isolation ... patterns suggest categories and rules, but these are immediate consequences of the text which exhibits them, without the *a priori* status they would hold in a grammar."[165] Goodman's notion of symbol systems has parallels to Lidov's notion of grammar. Both are approaches to deep structure that go beyond specific instances of symbols or marks, and instead capture something about the system as a whole. Goodman's theory is one of symbol systems, not symbols in isolation; the rules for these must extend to every possible element, not only the ones present in a text. Grammar is similarly universal in its reach, so that grammatical structures capture all possibilities. Grammar is specific to syntax, whereas symbol systems need not be.

---

[162] Lidov, *Elements of Semiotics*, 163.
[163] Also referred to as "paradigms," which concern semantics as on Saussure's axis of simultaneity and Jakobson's axis of equivalence.
[164] Lidov, *Elements of Semiotics*, 88.
[165] Lidov, *Elements of Semiotics*, 89.

Analytical perspectives using qualia and symbol systems are useful for looking at underlying frameworks and isolated graphics, but do not consider the syntactical relationships among notations within a given piece. Lidov outlines some additional components of grammar and pattern. Grammatical *categories* are "collections of possible constituents ... that are known to us but usually not all present to us; they are collections *in absentia*, and strictly in that sense abstract."[166] A grammatical category holds a single place on Jakobson's axis of combination but appeals to the possibilities afforded by the axis of selection. "A combination – a syntagm – that realizes a grammatical rule is a *form*."[167] Pattern is grounded in a specific text or work and does not need to appeal to the endless possibilities abstract grammatical categories and forms afford. Lidov further delineates *sets*, which are "paradigms determined by similarity and contrast within one text," and *units*, which are "syntagms determined by adjacency, parallelisms, and segmentation."[168] Grammar and pattern are both essential components to a well-informed interpretation of open notation.

In *TRAPPIST-1*, the pitch and time axes are grammatical structures. They are bound by rules that govern abstract qualities of the notations regardless of any specific marks in the score. These syntactical structures act as containers that can hold content; the pitch and time axes provide a plane upon which notation elements are placed. No matter how these elements appear, what qualia they afford, or their location on the page, the grammatical framework remains a constant; it transcends the specific with its global reach. The absence and presence of notations in the score constitutes another grammatical category. In *TRAPPIST-1*, the presence of notations indicates the presence of sound just as the absence of marks indicates the absence of sound. Asher's score is *descriptive* in that its notations visually describe the intended effect, rather than *prescribe* actions to create sounds.[169] Contrasting this are works by spectralist composers such as Jonathan Harvey, Tristan Murail, and Gérard Grisey, where attacks are shown with notes but without any visual indicator of the resulting resonance.[170] In these works, blank space in the score cannot be taken to indicate an absence of sound. Ironically, the blank space in the score is perhaps where the more interesting material occurs, as timbres shift and harmonics emerge in the sounds following attacks.

---

[166] Lidov, *Elements of Semiotics*, 164.

[167] Lidov, *Elements of Semiotics*, 164.

[168] Lidov, *Elements of Semiotics*, 165.

[169] Mieko Kanno, "Prescriptive Notation: Limits and Challenges," *Contemporary Music Review* 26, no. 2 (2007), 231–254.

[170] Marilyn Nonken, *The Spectral Piano: From Liszt, Scriabin, and Debussy to the Digital Age* (Cambridge: Cambridge University Press, 2014).

It is crucial to recognize that the grammar of *TRAPPIST-1* is mediated by the confluence of several elements: the composer, the score, and common practice. Asher perhaps consciously decided to consider time a function of the horizontal axis and pitch a function of the vertical, but this practice is evidenced by centuries of common practice. This orientation of time and pitch has become naturalized; it is evidence of a shared systematicity beyond the level of consciousness. The boundaries of the score also serve these grammatical categories; paper, which has only two dimensions that we make use of, easily supports a two-axis organization of information on a plane. It is also notable that Asher and I did not discuss this orientation; it was taken as a neutral and familiar foundation. By relying upon this frame, Asher guides the performer's attention away from complex decisions about timing and pitch (which are iconically conveyed in a familiar and natural-ized way), toward the qualia of her provocative and rich notations.

TRAPPIST-1 strongly relies upon pattern and emphasizes the individual perception of the performer as fertile ground for signifying musical material. Since pattern is evident within a single text, and merely suggests syntactical rules without needing to prove or support them globally, it is flexible and perceptually salient. For the performer developing an interpretation of an open score, pattern plays a significant role in reading syntactical structures. Take for example movement *b* (Figure 24).

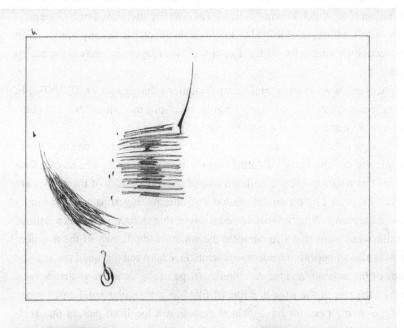

Figure 24 Leah Asher. *TRAPPIST-1* (2017), mov. *b*, p. 1

The movement begins with a small triangle slightly above the middle of the page. Five triangles in quick succession and tight horizontal placement return halfway through the movement. I interpreted the triangle notation to indicate unsustained pizzicato with fingernail. I disregarded the various orientations of the triangles, but another interpretation may regard that as a salient quality. I considered the variation in the size of the triangles to indicate relative dynamic level, so that the first, larger triangle is louder than the five following. Because pattern is a localized syntactical framework, these elements are not required to follow consistent rules that exist outside of the text as grammatical structures. This movement ends with a single dot near the top of the page, following a line that curves upward. For this movement, I considered small, isolated shapes to indicate pizzicato, regardless of shape. However, I read the difference in shape to indicate a difference in timbre. For the triangle notations, I read the sharpness of the triangles as indicative of a sharp timbre, which I achieved using the nail of my finger for the pizzicato. For the small dot, I used my fingertip to create a rounder timbre on the pizzicato. And since it is minuscule, I made that pizzicato as quiet as possible. The triangle notation returns in movement g (p. 13) and movement h (pp. 17–18, 21–22). I considered *TRAPPIST-1* a single piece and remained consistent in my interpretation of notations across movements. An interpretation that considered each movement in isolation would result in another layer of syntactical structures that relates pattern across different movements, which I do not believe was Asher's intention. For an interpretation of this nature, double syntax may become triple; ideas of pattern within individual movements would form an entirely new layer of syntax at the macro level.

Asher uses several other small-shape notations throughout *TRAPPIST-1*. In movement d, clusters of wavy, rectangular notations of various levels of completeness appear high on the page (Figure 25).

Although these rectangular notations share the small-shape element with the triangle and dot notations, I did not interpret them as pizzicati. The incompleteness of this notation and the hollowness and the low density of the shapes are perfectly captured by the sound created by fluttering fingertips over the tuning pegs of the piano. With the sustain pedal down, this technique creates a hollow, metallic sound, one that also captures the variations in density of the notation. There is also an appeal to the iconic resemblance between the small rectangular shape of the notation and the rectangular shape of the tuning pegs themselves. Toward the end of the page is a line of filled-in rectangular notations. I again used the tuning pegs for these, which maintains a localized pattern that rectangular notation indicates tuning pegs. I flicked them with the nail of my index

Figure 25 Leah Asher. *TRAPPIST-1* (2017), mov. *d*, p. 1

finger to create a heavier and more deliberate sound to parallel the heavy and bold qualities of the notation.

Another clear example of pattern is found on a page from movement *h*, which features a horizontal bar of circular notations of varying levels of completeness (Figure 26). Most of these circle notations are light, sketch-like, incomplete, and layered. Occasionally, sets of well-defined, dark, complete circles appear. Other unrelated notations appear above and below this material, such as a solitary triangle.

The horizontal bar of circle notation is a unique and defining element of movement *h* that runs through most of its eight pages, so I incorporated an extended technique unique to this movement. With one hand I held a rubber tuning mute to the middle register of the strings of the piano, and with the other hand I played the corresponding keys. The result was a muted, indistinct, dull sound that paralleled those qualities of the notation. I did not attempt an iconic and isomorphic reading of the number of indistinct circles, as I felt that would be excessively meticulous. Instead, I followed the relative density and contour of the notation as indicators of relative density and pitch. Toward the middle of this excerpt, the indistinct circle notation thins to a single line; in this area, I played just one or two notes under the mute, whereas in other areas the notes

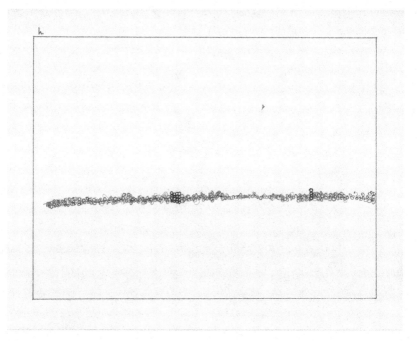

Figure 26 Leah Asher. *TRAPPIST-1* (2017), mov. *h*, p. 1

I played spanned a fourth or fifth. I attempted to play streams of irregular notes for the indistinct circle notations that evoked a kind of clanging texture. For the areas with well-defined circles, I played percussive and clear notes that did iconically correspond to the number of circles. This division of pitch articulation parallels the visual distinctness of the circles on the page. For the first group on this page, there are four sets of four vertically stacked circles; I played four four-note chords, clearly articulated, and yet still dulled by the tuning mute.

This reading of pattern involves *sets*, which are "paradigms determined by similarity and contrast within one text."[171] Pattern contrasts with grammar in that it does not demand global adherence. Patterns can be locally perceived within a text and are perhaps more obvious to the receiver as a syntactical element.

> Patterns are discovered by abduction or induction. Pattern is known only *a posteriori* in relation to the text and develops from perceptions of symmetries of all kinds: repetitions, variations, and transformations and contrasts . . .
> In principle, we do not need to know about a particular set before we encounter it and recognize it as such.[172]

171 Lidov, *Elements of Semiotics*, 165.
172 Lidov, *Elements of Semiotics*, 165.

Pattern sets are key to developing readings of scores like *TRAPPIST-1* that are consistent throughout. As demonstrated in the prior examples, it is through recognizing similarity and contrast within notational paradigms that the performer develops an interpretation that is not a random and improvised collection of sounds, but a palette of sound rooted in the text. In practice, this involves abductively or inductively developing an understanding of structures within a piece. In works such as *TRAPPIST-1* where virtually no explanation of notations is given to limit the interpretation, this can seem daunting. Yet with every decision, the array of possibilities for other elements is further constrained. For example, with the small-shape notations, I first noticed the pattern by simply observing the notations without playing. Once I decided to consider small-shape notations as pizzicato sounds, two things were accomplished: it defined one parameter of the pattern set and limited the interpretation of contrasting material. If small shapes were to indicate pizzicati, other shapes should not. Building an interpretation of notations based on individual qualities is semantic work, and building an interpretation of notations across the space and time structures of the score is syntactic work. The performer must mediate between both semantic and syntactic domains throughout the process of learning, rehearsing, and performing openly notated works.

4 Final Thoughts

In Section 3.3, I showed how *TRAPPIST-1* relies upon grammar and pattern as two components of double syntax. It is only through developing and reconciling pattern sets with overarching grammatical categories that the performer can successfully navigate the syntax of this work. This is also true for Redman's *Book* and Brown's *Folio*. Despite Redman's emphasis on the "unsystematic" nature of *Book*, structural and syntactical elements remain salient features of the work. To interpret any score, the performer connects visual signs in the score with musical objects in their mind by way of interpretants in the Peircean sense. This process is not randomly conducted for each sign, but mediated by various syntactical elements in the score. *Book* challenges the grammar of conventional notation through several compositional and notational strategies: the performer is denied any firm grounding in conventional grammatical categories through erasure and oversaturation, and with extension, the grammatical function of the staff is subverted by extending the notational capacity of the staff as an expressive graphic notation. By contrast, certain grammatical categories in Brown's *November 1952* and *December 1952* are well defined either through overlap with conventional notations or through instructional material. One example would be the notation of pitch in *November 1952*, which is shared with conventional notation. In this system, the grammatical category of pitch represents every possible pitch that could be notated on the staff. In *December 1952*, Brown gives examples of possible applications of musical parameters to visual parameters of the score. For example, the horizontal axis can isomorphically relate to the passage of time. In this way, the horizontal axis is a grammatical category in that it represents all possible moments in time for the piece. Brown promotes consistency within the interpretation of these works while maintaining a high degree of openness in interpretation.

Redman's desire to thrust the performer into a "wilderness of self-sufficiency" is furthered by his denial of structural grammatical elements. Stable elements inevitably rupture or transform; in conventionally notated music, instability and rupture might be signified by dissonant harmonies, contrasting musical material, and loud dynamics. In *Book*, Redman conveys this through the visual presentation of his notations. Open notations often involve intentional disruption of grammatical categories and therefore the deeper structural organization. Despite Redman's best efforts to disorient the performer, some grammatical elements remain intact. When the staff is in a more conventional orientation, vestiges of its conventional grammar remain. Even when some elements such as clef or staff lines are removed, deeper structural elements are not. The mapping of pitch to the vertical axis, for example, may be present even when the staff lines are gone. In a similar fashion, while oversaturation may obstruct grammatical elements such as connections among noteheads and pitches, qualities such as density of pitch material are still evident and meaningful. This is not to say that Redman fails to limit the grasp of grammatical structure; he does. In *Book*, there is a much stronger emphasis on syntactical meaning making through pattern. Similar to how performers must build pattern sets to make a meaningful and consistent interpretation of *TRAPPIST-1*, performers must create some guidelines for navigating through *Book*. Redman's conception of a musical "genetics" is a syntactical design that exists at the crossroads of grammar and pattern.[173] *Book* disorients the performer by attempting to dislodge and disrupt conventional grammatical elements adapted from standard notations, and to some extent it succeeds. More so, these notations ask that the performer create localized meaning through the perception of pattern sets, such as density, absence, and proximity.

The analysis of symbol systems, sign-types, and syntactical structures reveals much about the performance implications of Asher's *TRAPPIST-1*. The performer who considers these semiotic elements can make informed decisions while crafting an interpretation of the score. I illustrate how this

---

[173] Redman, "Scroll."

analytical work supports a meaningful performance through examples of my own working process. *TRAPPIST-1* uses symbol systems to convey pitch and time on the vertical and horizontal axes, respectively; they are analog symbol systems, as they chart pitch and time continuously along each axis. However, similar to Brown's *December 1952*, the analogicity of the notations can be ignored in practice in favor of a more general and relative interpretation. Asher's notations are abstract in that they do not reference the lexicon of standard notations. Instead, the hand-drawn notations are imbued with various qualities that the performer reads by way of qualic transitivity. Visual qualities such as darkness, sharpness, density, and shape are considered prescient indicators of musical objects. Syntactical analysis shows grammar and pattern as both contributing to the structure of the piece. Grammatical elements include the representation of pitch and time on axes, which parallels the universal reach of analog symbol systems. The performer perceives pattern locally as instances of contrast, similarity, and repetition. In order to develop a consistent and meaningful interpretation, the performer must develop pattern sets that are applicable for the piece as a whole, a process often informed by qualia. In the same way that qualia indicate musical potential for individual notations, they contribute to the mapping of pattern across the entirety of the piece.

The semiotic analysis of open works does not just produce interesting discrepancies across pieces, but provides the means for deep and meaningful interpretation. It may be tempting to assume that anything goes for open notations, or that an improvisational approach offers the same end product as a thoughtful interpretation. And yet, without understanding the inner workings of open notations and their contexts, this approach will produce haphazard results. Just as an interpretation that is given little thought can misrepresent the notations in a score, an interpretation that is meticulously crafted can also miss the mark. The care and attention given to the interpretation of standardly notated musical works should be matched for works with open notations. It is the performer's responsibility to understand the boundaries and limitations to their freedom when working with open notations, so that the interpretive decisions they make remain within the scope of the work the composer intended.

Appendix
Prompts for Analysis

This appendix is a concise set of prompts for analyzing works with open notations with a semiotic eye. As a preliminary exercise, consider the following musical parameters as they relate to the score in question:

- Pitch
- Dynamics
- Durations/Rhythm
- Timbre
- Sequence of Events

It may be helpful to describe in writing how each of these elements appears in the score before trying to answer the following prompts. If you are a performer, or consider the perspective of the performer in your analysis, walk through how you might read, transcribe, or generate sound material for each musical parameter before proceeding. Certain questions or prompts may not be applicable or may not produce interesting results for the specific work you analyze – this is meant to be a starting point, not a checklist of questions to produce a complete analysis. Instead, focus on the questions and prompts that give you complex responses; push deeper into these areas to develop a nuanced and deep analysis.

Consider the following questions for each musical parameter just listed:

- What information is present, and conversely, what information is absent in the score?
- For the information that is present, how is it organized?
- What information aligns with a conventional or familiar notation scheme?
- What information subverts your expectations?
- More generally, is there a dominant mode of reading at work? (Mitchell)
- For each parameter, how is weight assigned to the iconic, indexical, and symbolic modes? (Peirce)
- Does each musical parameter encourage systematicity, or defy an overarching logic? If so, does analysis as analog/digital system reveal anything? (Goodman)
- Does the parameter encourage engagement with syntactic pattern and grammar in a particular way? (Lidov)

For each ambiguous musical parameter:

- Does the openness of the musical parameter encourage the performer to assign value to qualia? (Harkness/Chumley)
- Is there an isomorphic or iconic resemblance between a measurable element in the score and a corresponding musical parameter?
- Does the composer employ recurring compositional strategies that contribute to the openness of the notation?

Extra-notational information to consider:

- What are the markers of a successful performance or realization of the piece, and what informs this sense of *Werktreue*? (Goehr)
- How has entextualization contributed to your understanding of the piece? (Urban)
  - Consider direct information from the composer, such as emails, workshops, rehearsals, and recorded interviews.
  - Consider the influence of prior performances such as recordings, markings in the score, or verbal instructions from another performer.
- Is there a clear division between the composer and the performer? If not, what roles are played, enforced, or encouraged by the social context surrounding the work?

Bibliography

Asher, Leah, "Home Page." Leah Asher official website. Accessed December 17, 2019. www.leahasher.com.

Asher, Leah, *TRAPPIST-1* (Independently published, 2017).

Brent, Joseph, *Charles Sanders Peirce: A Life* (Bloomington: Indiana University Press, 1993).

Brown, Earle, *FOLIO (1952/53) and 4 Systems (1954)* (New York: Associated Music, 1961).

Brown, Earle, "The Notation and Performance of New Music," *Musical Quarterly* 72, no.2 (1986), 180–201.

Brown, Earle, "On December 1952," [1970; transcription of audio] *American Music* 26, no. 1 (Spring 2008), 1–12.

Brown, Earle, "Prefatory Note," in *FOLIO (1952/53) and 4 Systems (1954)* (New York: Associated Music, 1961).

Byrd, Donald, "Extremes of Conventional Music Notation," Indiana University Bloomington. Revised mid-October 2018. Accessed December 17, 2019. http://homes.soic.indiana.edu/donbyrd/CMNExtremes.htm

Cady, Jason, "An Overview of Earle Brown's Techniques and Media," in *Beyond Notation: The Music of Earle Brown*, edited by Rebecca Y. Kim (Ann Arbor: University of Michigan Press, 2017), 1–20.

Cage, John, *Notations*, edited by Alison Knowles and John Cage (New York: Something Else Press, 1969).

Chandler, Daniel, *Semiotics: The Basics*, 2nd edition (London: Routledge, 2002).

Chumley, Lily, and Nicholas Harkness, "Introduction: QUALIA," *Anthropological Theory* 13, no. 1–2 (2013), 3–11.

Cowell, Henry, "Explanation of Symbols and Playing Instructions," in *Piano Music by Henry Cowell* (New York: Associated Music, 1960).

Eco, Umberto, *The Open Work*, translated by Anna Cancogni (Cambridge, MA: Harvard University Press, 1989).

Goehr, Lydia, "Being True to the Work," *Journal of Aesthetics and Art Criticism* 47, no.1 (Winter 1989), 55–67.

Goehr, Lydia, *The Imaginary Museum of Musical Works*, revised edition (London: Oxford University Press, 2007).

Goodman, Nelson, *Languages of Art* [1968], new edition (Indianapolis, IN: Hackett, 1976).

Gresser, Clemens, "Earle Brown's 'Creative Ambiguity' and Ideas of Co-creatorship in Selected Works," *Contemporary Music Review* 26, no. 3/4 (June/August 2007), 377–394.

Harkness, Nicholas, "Softer Soju in South Korea," *Anthropological Theory* 13, no. 1–2 (2013), 12–30.

Harkness, Nicholas, *Songs of Seoul: An Ethnography of Voice and Voicing in Christian South Korea* (Berkeley: University of California Press, 2014).

Hoover, Elizabeth, "Collage and the Feedback Condition of Earle Brown's *Calder Piece*," in *Beyond Notation: The Music of Earle Brown*, edited by Rebecca Y. Kim (Ann Arbor: University of Michigan Press, 2017), 159–187.

Jakobson, Roman, "Closing Statement: Linguistics and Poetics," in *Style in Language*, edited by Thomas A. Sebeok (Cambridge: MIT Press, 1960), 350–377.

Kanno, Mieko, "Prescriptive Notation: Limits and Challenges," *Contemporary Music Review* 26, no. 2 (2007), 231–254.

Karkoschka, Erhard, *Notation in New Music: A Critical Guide to Interpretation and Realization*, translated by Ruth Koenig (New York: Praeger, 1972).

Kulvicki, John, "Analog Representation and the Parts Principle," *Review of Philosophy and Psychology* 6 (2015), 165–180.

Lévi-Strauss, Claude, *Structural Anthropology*, translated by Claire Jacobson and Brooke Grundfest Schoepf (New York: Basic Books, 1963).

Lidov, David, *Elements of Semiotics: A Neo-structuralist Perspective*, 2nd edition (2017). https://davidlidov.com/about/elements-of-semiotics-2017/

Mavromatis, Panayotis, "A Multi-tiered Approach for Analyzing Expressive Timing in Musical Performance," in *Mathematics and Computation in Music*, edited by Elaine Chew, Adrian Childs, and Ching-Hua Chuan (Berlin: Springer, 2009), 193–204.

McKay, Tristan, "Graphic Notations As Creative Resilience in Redman's *Book* (2006)," in *Semiotics 2018: Resilience in an Age of Relation*, edited by Geoffrey Ross Owens and Elvira Katić (Charlottesville, VA: Philosophy Documentation Center Press, 2019), 157–171.

Merrell, Floyd, "Charles Sanders Peirce's Concept of the Sign," in *The Routledge Companion to Semiotics and Linguistics*, edited by Paul Cobley (London: Routledge, 2001), 28–39.

Mitchell, W. J. T, "Pictures and Paragraphs: Nelson Goodman," in *Iconology: Image, Text, Ideology* (Chicago: University of Chicago Press, 1986), 47–74.

Munn, Nancy D, *The Fame of Gawa: A Symbolic Study of Value Transformation in a Massim (Papua New Guinea) Society* (Cambridge: Cambridge University Press, 1986).

Nonken, Marilyn, *The Spectral Piano: From Liszt, Scriabin, and Debussy to the Digital Age* (Cambridge: Cambridge University Press, 2014).

Parmentier, Richard, *Signs in Society: Studies in Semiotic Anthropology* (Indianapolis: Indiana University Press, 1994).

Peirce, Charles S., Charles Hartshorne, Paul Weiss, and Arthur W. Burks, *Collected Papers of Charles Sanders Peirce* (Cambridge, MA: Belknap Press of Harvard University Press, 1965).

The Peirce Edition Project, "History" (2015). Accessed December 17, 2019. http://peirce.iupui.edu/#history

The Peirce Edition Project, "Welcome to the Peirce Edition Project" (2015). Accessed December 17, 2019. http://peirce.iupui.edu/index.html

Redman, Will, "Book," Will Redman official website (2006). Accessed December 17, 2019. www.willredman.com/book.html

Redman, Will, "Deck," Will Redman official website (2016). Accessed December 17, 2019. www.willredman.com/deck.html

Redman, Will, "Honoring Vertical Excellence," Will Redman official website (2011). Accessed December 17, 2019. www.willredman.com/hve.html

Redman, Will, "Long Bio," Will Redman official website (2010). Accessed December 17, 2019. www.willredman.com/long_bio.html

Redman, Will, "Scroll," Will Redman official website (2016). Accessed December 17, 2019. www.willredman.com/scroll.html

Redman, Will, "Short Bio," Will Redman official website (2010). Accessed December 17, 2019. www.willredman.com/short_bio.html

Redman, Will, "Will Redman: Graphic Ideas in Sound," video interview by Molly Sheridan, *New Music Box* (blog) (July 27, 2011). Accessed December 17, 2019. https://vimeo.com/26929349

Robey, David, Introduction to *The Open Work*, by Umberto Eco (Cambridge, MA: Harvard University Press, 1989), vii–xxxii.

Ruwet, Nicholas, and Mark Everist, "Methods of Analysis in Musicology," *Music Analysis* 6, no. 1/2 (March–July 1987), 3–9, 11–36.

Sauer, Theresa, *Notations 21* (New York: Mark Batty, 2009).

de Saussure, Ferdinand, *Course in General Linguistics* [1916], new edition translated by Roy Harris (La Salle, IL: Open Court, 1986).

Tormey, Alan, "Indeterminacy and Identity in Art," *The Monist* 58, no. 2 (April 1974), 203–215.

Tufte, Edward R., *The Visual Display of Quantitative Information*, (Cheshire, CT: Graphics Press, 1983).

Tullett, Barrie, *Typewriter Art: A Modern Anthology* (London: Laurence King, 2014).

University of Chicago, "History," Department of Anthropology. Accessed December 17, 2019. https://anthropology.uchicago.edu/about-us/history

Urban, Greg, "Entextualization, Replication, and Power," in *Natural Histories of Discourse*, edited by Michael Silverstein and Greg Urban (Chicago: University of Chicago Press, 1996), 21–44.

Waugh, Linda, "The Poetic Function in the Theory of Roman Jakobson," *Poetics Today* 2, no. 1a (Autumn 1980), 57–82.

Acknowledgments

This Element is adapted from my PhD dissertation (New York University, May 2019), and as such I owe my deep gratitude to my chair, Marilyn Nonken, and committee member Lily Chumley. Thank you to my deeply insightful external readers Panayotis Mavromatis and Nicholas Harkness, and to David Lidov and Elizabeth Hoffman for their mentorship at various stages of my research. Finally, thank you to the Semiotic Society of America and the NOVA Contemporary Music Meeting for opportunities to present earlier versions of this work.

Cambridge Elements ≡

Music since 1945

Mervyn Cooke
University of Nottingham

Mervyn Cooke brings to the role of series editor an unusually broad range of expertise, having published widely in the fields of twentieth-century opera, concert and theatre music, jazz, and film music. He has edited and co-edited *Cambridge Companions to Britten, Jazz, Twentieth-Century Opera*, and *Film Music*. His other books include *Britten: War Requiem, Britten and the Far East, A History of Film Music, The Hollywood Film Music Reader, Pat Metheny: The ECM Years*, and two illustrated histories of jazz. He is currently co-editing (with Christopher R. Wilson) *The Oxford Handbook of Shakespeare and Music*.

About the Series

Elements in Music since 1945 is a highly stimulating collection of authoritative online essays that reflects the latest research into a wide range of musical topics of international significance since the Second World War. Individual Elements are organised into constantly evolving clusters devoted to such topics as art music, jazz, music and image, stage and screen genres, music and media, music and place, immersive music, music and movement, music and politics, music and conflict, and music and society. The latest research questions in theory, criticism, musicology, composition and performance are also given cutting-edge and thought-provoking coverage. The digital-first format allows authors to respond rapidly to new research trends, with contributions being updated to reflect the latest thinking in their fields, and the essays are enhanced by the provision of an exciting range of online resources.

Cambridge Elements ≡

Music since 1945

Elements in the Series

Printed in the United States
by Baker & Taylor Publisher Services